Let's Whittinghill Again
(Like We Did Last Summer)

Let's Whittinghill Again
(Like We Did Last Summer)

Dick Whittinghill
with Don Page

cbi **Contemporary Books, Inc.**
Chicago

Library of Congress Cataloging in Publication Data

Whittinghill, Dick.
    Let's Whittinghill again (like we did last summer).

    Autobiographical.
    Includes index.
    1. Whittinghill, Dick.   2. Disc jockeys—United
States—Biography.   I. Page, Don, joint author.
II. Title.
ML429.W44A33   789.9'1 [B]   77-75842
ISBN 0-8092-7742-5

Published by Contemporary Books, Inc.
180 North Michigan Avenue, Chicago, Illinois 60601
Manufactured in the United States of America
Library of Congress Catalog Card Number: 77-75842
International Standard Book Number: 0-8092-7742-5

Published simultaneously in Canada by
Beaverbooks
953 Dillingham Road
Pickering, Ontario L1W 1Z7
Canada

For my wife, WILAMET
Only *she* knows what Whittinghilling *really* means

Contents

Foreword

WE WERE RETURNING in Paul Caruso's royal purple Rolls-Royce from a holiday golfing expedition in Fillmore, California, when Dick Whittinghill began to regale us again with more stories of his escapades in radioland.

Of course, we were howling. And remember, we're a tough jury. On board were Caruso, who is Beverly Hills's most renowned Sicilian attorney; Bob Forward, the actor and former program director of KMPC radio; Jim Murray, the award-winning, nationally syndicated sports columnist of the *Los Angeles Times*; Roger Leighton, ex-fight manager who serves as Caruso's bodyguard, chauffeur, and man Friday; myself (the career journalist); and Old Whit.

We had our quota of shooters on the course, and we were loose, you might say. Whit was a bit looser. As we tooled toward the San Fernando Valley and our eventual destination, Lakeside Golf Club (the bar), I began taking notes. Actually, I was jotting down chapter headings.

"Why didn't you include some of these stories in your first book, Dick?" Caruso wondered.

"Oh, I just didn't think of them," he answered. "I thought of so many, and then more things have happened since the book came out—you know, the usual crazy things, the screw-ups—that I could probably do another book." Whit added the last line in jest, but the little light had already gone on in my head.

By the time we were seated at the round table at Lakeside ordering more shooters, I had a whole note pad full of chapter ideas. By the end of the evening I showed them to Dick and said, "When do we start on the next book?"

Our jolly group immediately seconded the notion and Hollywood's favorite pixie disc jockey was swept up in the tide of our enthusiasm.

"Do you really think people will buy another one?" he asked, with typical modesty.

"You bet they will," Jim Murray said, earnestly.

"When do we start?" Whit inquired.

"We never stopped," I said.

In *Did You Whittinghill This Morning?*—still available at bookstores—we were introduced to the Kid from Montana, and we traveled with him from the small town of Helena to the big town of New York and on to New Guinea and Japan and Glendale and Hollywood. We also learned of his near-record list of jobs and terminations. And we met the Lakeside gang and all of the other characters who have danced in and out of Whit's colorful life.

But there is so much more, and so here Whit will fill in some spaces left out in past adventures and bring us up-to-date with many new tales. This account, I believe, is as funny all the way through as the first one but with more of Whit personally in it and some serious moments that you should find rewarding, informative, and even touching.

But prepare for another madcap ride, and hold on tight because we're moving fast again!

Don Page

1

Here We Go Again, Funsters!

"THANK YOU VERY MUCH for listening, now if you'll excuse me . . ."

That's how I end my morning show every day and that's how we ended our last adventure together—but, as you can see, I'm back again. Yes, I'm back because I'm a natural born loudmouth and this, I suspect, is what has kept me on the air at the same station (KMPC) for 27 years.

Within this lengthy period, I've seen a bigger personnel turnover than the Republican party. Guys have retired, died, left the radio business to sell real estate and tend bar, a few have been fired, and some ran away with another woman. Me? I'm still here playing records, saying silly things, having a few shooters, playing golf, and going home to Willy. And she's still patient with me.

Remember last time when I told you about the *younger* fellow who was brought in from the East years ago to wait in the wings in the event of my retirement or death? Remember how I told you he waits in the hallway every morning to take my pulse? Well, he doesn't do that anymore. Instead he's drinking what I drink, but he's looking *older* than me every day. By the time I'm ready to retire, they're going to have to find a replacement for *him*.

One thing has changed drastically since our last visit. My golf game has gone bad and I'm up to a 17 handicap now. It wasn't too long ago that I played to a comfortable 12. My swing was always kind of quaint, but I hit the ball straight and my putting was good. Now my swing is a little better and I hit harder, but it's taking me longer to get there. Funny thing, though, I'm in the best shape of my adult life, almost as good as I was when I was playing football at Helena High. I play golf at Lakeside twice a week and go to a gym in North Hollywood three times a week—and it's jammy time by 9:30 P.M.

So why is my golf game going sour? Maybe it's the Shack.

The Shack is a little food and beverage stand on hole No. 15. On a hot day (or even a cold one) our foursomes always pause at the Shack for a rest and a sip of something for medicinal purposes. This is where my game seems to fade and I come into 18 with lead in my shoes. Thinking it over lately, I realize it's on 15 that my opponents start to press or renegotiate our rules.

Anyway, enough of this at the moment—we'll have more tales of the Lakeside woods later in our tour.

Being a loudmouth I never run out of stories, and sitting around with the gang watching the sun set over No. 9 at Lakeside, I've been reminded often of stories I left out of the first book. Then, too, more ridiculous things have happened (almost daily) since then—and I'm still toddling through life under a little gray cloud on a banana peel.

In this attempt, let us begin with my triumphant return to Ireland, the home of my grandparents and where I once asked Barry Fitzgerald to go to mass with me only to find out that he was Protestant!

Pour yourself a little of the *hard* and we'll be off.

2

Return to Ireland
(oh, to be in Sneem,
now that spring is here . . .)

I RELAND WASN'T READY FOR US—a'tal, a'tal, a'tal!

It was a great group—Bert West, president of Golden West Broadcasters; Don Ross, who puts on my charity golf tournament; Bill Hipple, public relations director of American Airlines; and the Kid from Montana. Last year, despite all the problems with the IRA, *we* invaded Ireland. Lakeside's version of the Fearsome Foursome.

London was the first stop, and all I remember about London is that they must hire some guy to switch all of the water faucets around—the hot and cold are reversed from ours—and to hide the toilet paper. What I'll always remember about London is that you can't reach the toilet paper from a sitting position.

When we arrived at Shannon Airport we were met by Fergus, a driver commissioned by Hipple to take us on a tour of the Irish golf courses. As we motored to our hotel, the Old Ground, I thought of my grandparents and Barry Fitzgerald and I got a lump in my throat. We went to dinner and Fergus jumped right in with us, lapping up the booze and eating with both hands while he gave us a quick and interesting history of the Old Sod. He spoke Gaelic and a couple of other languages and everyone in town seemed to know him, so I figured we were in capable hands.

The next day Fergus took us to a hurling match in the small town of Tulla. There was no grandstand, no bleachers, nothing. Just a big field with spectators standing all around. It was shoulder to shoulder and I soon discovered that the Irish hadn't heard about underarm deodorant, and this shirt-sleeve crowd was gamey!

Hurling is like an organized prison riot and very hard to follow.

"Hipple, you know anything about this game?"

"Never saw it before, Whit."

"How about you, Bert?"

"I think it's something like cricket."

"No," said Ross, "it's like lacrosse."

I would have asked Fergus, but he was off having a schooner of stout at the nearby pub.

Well, we soon found out that hurling is mayhem! The players have these little bats and they hit the ball all around, and I couldn't figure out how it was scored. It seemed you got three points for hitting the ball over the goal and five points for beating a guy on the knee. There was no scoreboard, either. Periodically, they'd stop the game and a kid would run out with a bucket of water for both teams. Then they'd start again, hitting the ball up in the air and whacking each other's heads as it came down. People were falling down all over the place.

I had a bet with Hipple, so I began asking the spectators what the score was? I asked one guy who was cheering wildly and jumping up and down and waving his arms.

"Have no idea, sport," he said. He cheered even louder when some poor guy got his head cracked. It suddenly dawned on me that all these people were here to watch skulls split.

Later, in the local pub, I'm still trying to find out who won. I'm asking the bar patrons and nobody knew. Finally, I found one of the players who was gulping down a pint of stout through his puffed-up lips and shattered teeth. (Whew! He didn't know about deodorant, either.)

"Damned if I know, luv."

Even the *players* didn't know.

We're cruising through the countryside with Fergus telling us more stories about Ireland and occasionally punctuating his remarks with "Confusion to England" when I cup my hand to the side of my mouth and whisper, "IRA?" Hipple, Ross, and West look over at Fergus and they all nod. So, I think to myself, here we are in Ireland, complete strangers, and our driver is a member of the Irish Republican Army. We're all going to get shot.

But I put this out of my mind when we come to a little fork in the road and a sign that reads "Sneem."

"Stop here, Fergus!"

"Why are we stopping here, Whit?" Hipple inquired. "There's nothing here."

"We've got to stop in Sneem," I said. "We've got to tell people back home that we stopped in Sneem. It sounds like something you'd get on your pants. You've got *Sneem* all over you . . ."

Here's the tableau:

Sneem, Ireland, is only two blocks long. It has two churches, a police station—and 17 bars!

We get out of the car, and both sides of the street are lined with bars. So we pick one and go in and everyone in the place is stoned out of his gourd! Men are dancing with men! There are children in the place, too.

"Let's get out of here," I whisper to Hipple and Hipple whispers to Ross and West.

Now we're in the pub next door and the same thing is going on. Everyone is absolutely fractured. And it's this way all over town!

So we go across the street and here's a guy lurching out of another bar, careening off a couple of parked cars and staggering to the middle of the street where he suddenly throws his head to the left and throws up over his shoulder and never misses stride. It's the first time I've ever seen a guy throw up on the fly!

Now we're in the saloon the guy lurched out of and it's the same. Women and children and the men are all drunk, men are dancing with men, and there's this guy playing an accordion and he's smashed and his fingers are grabbing the keys, not playing chords, and you hear ounchhh-ounchhh and people are *dancing* to it. Everybody's loving it.

Finally, I sidled up to a fellow who looked half-sober and I asked him, "Just what do you do in this town?"

"Oh, we drink a little and farm a little and drink a little . . ."

He orders another "jar of the hard." In Ireland whisky is the *hard*. And I ordered a jar of the hard, which is Paddy's—the best Irish whisky of them all.

Oh, I forgot, by this time we've had a short conference and voted out Fergus. Fergus didn't seem to understand he was our driver, not a member of the party. He had been freeloading on us all the way and it had to stop since there were so many bars in Ireland. Reluctantly, he was paying his own way now or sitting in the car.

We head back for the car and experience one final vignette. Here comes a citizen in an old sedan, weaving along the street, and coming to an abrupt halt in front of a pub. The door opens and this guy falls out on the road. He crawls to his feet and staggers into the bar, leaving his motor running.

We said good-bye to Sneem—but it was too drunk to acknowledge it.

We forged ahead to Lahinch, a seaside golf course with sand

dunes and grass up to your hips if you hit the ball in the rough. All four courses we played were like this; I never saw anything like it. When we teed off, two goats were watching us. In fact, we found out later, they keep goats on the courses to keep the grass from spreading like a runaway infection.

The fairways, if you could call them that, were six yards across and you had no idea where the hole was. We would send Fergus ahead to mark the hole: "You take the point, Fergus." And he'd be standing way up on a mountain, a lonely little figure. It was like watching "Combat."

Strangely enough, under these horrible conditions, the courses were always packed and most of the golfers had surprisingly good swings. Me? I never got out of the tall grass.

After Lahinch, the next stop was Waterville Lake Hotel, owned by John A. Mulcahy of Palm Springs, California—and he owns half of the Springs, too. Actually the place is an old castle and we had a sumptuous feast that night and during dinner the subject of fishing came up. We heard what fine fishing is available in this picturesque part of Ireland.

I'm not much of a fisherman, but Hipple and Ross claim they're experts and they're talking about the proper bait to use for certain fish and telling tall stories of catching big ones, when Mulcahy pipes up, "Fellas, I'm sorry but there are no fish in the lake. The British dammed up the front end of it so the fish couldn't get through."

"Confusion to England," Fergus says, raising his pint of stout.

The next day we go fishing anyway. Ross and I are in one boat, Bert is in another boat, and Hipple is with a 15-year-old guide named Paddy, who is also rowing him.

We go for two or three hours hoping to catch something, and the clean, fresh air and the beer and the swaying boats are beginning to make us groggy, so we stop for a little picnic on a small island on the lake.

Now we're munching on sandwiches and drinking beer and

touring the island. It has monastery ruins from the twelfth century and the rock ruins of a prayer house from the fifth century. And I notice a tiny grave with a skeleton in it and goats standing all around. Suddenly, I feel stupid. Here's a guy standing in front of a grave with a skeleton, eating a sandwich and drinking beer with a bunch of goats staring at him.

Rowing back to the hotel we sense something's wrong.

"Where is Hipple?" Ross asks.

"I don't know," I said. "Wasn't he at the grave with us?"

"No, I didn't see him or the kid," Ross replies.

"Hey, Bert!" Ross yells. "You seen Hipple?"

"Yeah, he was about 100 yards behind us five minutes ago, but it looked like he was headed in the opposite direction."

Opposite direction?

It was about an hour after we got back to the hotel when Hipple showed up. He looked tired and windblown.

"Where the hell have you been, Hip?"

"Oh, that kid's parents gave me a terrific lecture," he said, wearily.

"Lecture?"

"Yeah, for getting Paddy smashed."

"You mean the guide—the *kid*?!"

"Yeah."

It seems that Hipple took all the beer and put it in his boat after the picnic and shared it with the 15-year-old kid.

"He got so drunk, I had to do the rowing," Hipple complained. "We were going around in circles."

"How'd his parents react?" Bert wondered.

"Jeez, they were mad," Hipple says. "I took him home to his little thatched-roof house, you know, I didn't want him walking home alone in his condition. But his parents got mad as hell and gave me a lecture on morals, I guess. I don't know. Bartender, I'll have some of the hard," he added.

"Bill, why would you get a 15-year-old kid drunk?" I scolded.

Hipple can't figure out where he went wrong. "Well, if

there's beer in the boat shouldn't everybody share?"

(Here, I must insert the fact that children *do* drink in Ireland. Kids five, six and seven go to the pubs with their parents like family day, and they drink a mixture of half-lemonade and half-beer called *shandy*. It doesn't seem to bother them because all the kids I saw were laughin' a lot.)

All through Ireland you see road signs that warn: ALCOHOL HARMS DRIVING. We made a note of that and made sure that Fergus was off the hard while driving.

As we went from town to town, we also noticed—with some concern—that none of the Irish women wore bras (Erin, no bra!). And coming into Killarney for golf at Killarney Golf & Fishing Club we made a pit stop at Glenbeigh Village. There we saw a remarkable sight. A woman with a nice figure stepped out of the pub at the Towers Hotel and started across the street in front of the car. Remember, they never heard of silicones in Ireland.

She would have made Sophia Loren look like Don Knotts!

She could have nursed Wisconsin.

Fergus is telling us about this lovely little place called Port Laoise where, coincidentally, they have a prison for IRA members. It happens to be on the way to Dublin, our final destination. "Well, let's get some pictures of it," Hipple demands, sipping the hard.

Just slightly off the main road, Port Laoise is indeed an emerald green and sunny spot, a place where a painter would like to live. Fergus scratches his beard and reveals that a big breakout was attempted just recently and the town was a bit nervous.

But Hipple isn't nervous. He slides out of the car and trains his camera on one of the prison's turrets. We notice a couple of Irish soldiers looking back at us through binoculars. Slowly, one of the soldiers turns a machine gun in our direction. With Hipple in the lead, we scrambled back into the limousine like fleeing bank robbers.

Dead tired, we near the end of our journey, staying overnight at the Gresham Hotel on O'Connell Street.

We've been in the car a long time and playing a lot of golf, and by now Bert West's bad back is really hurting him. Unfortunately, there are no masseurs on duty late at night at the hotel. Bert is in pain.

"I can fix your back," Hipple says. "I give the world's greatest massage."

We have a close-knit group, but I never knew this about Hipple. I never knew he got 15-year-old kids smashed, either.

So we follow Hipple up to Bert's room and Bert can hardly get up the stairs. Hipple tells him to take off his clothes, wrap a towel around his middle, and stretch out on the bed.

Hipple disappears for a few minutes, then comes back in a costume—a massage outfit, which consists of sandals and a little robe with "Nagoya Hotel" written on it.

I was amazed.

"Face down on the bed, Bert," Hipple commands. Bert does and Hipple starts to massage—very professionally, I thought.

"Wait a minute," Hipple says, stopping abruptly. "I don't have any oil, or anything moist for my hands."

And I think, big deal, you got the Nagoya thing on and you're supposed to be a massager. Why don't you have all of your equipment?

"I left out that one thing in packing," he says.

Hipple disappears again.

Now I'm consoling Bert. "Don't worry, Bert, he's got *sandals*—he must be the greatest."

Hipple returns and he has this white lubricant in his hands. And he starts massaging Bert's back and Bert is groaning and getting a lot of pleasure out of it. Everything seems fine and Bert falls asleep, smiling.

The next morning we're having breakfast and I notice that Bert is kind of squirming around in his chair and scratching his back and mumbling.

"What did you use to give Bert that massage?" I ask Hipple, who is nibbling blissfully on some berries.

"Oh," he says, drying his mouth, "I used toothpaste. Only thing I had."

Well, the toothpaste had hardened on Bert's back and he couldn't scrub it off. For three days, he was doing a combination Irish jig and bugaloo.

On our last day, we stumble into Dublin's famous The Bailey, which was a popular watering hole for rascals like James Joyce and Brendan Behan. We're not in the bar five minutes when I hear a voice from the rear of the room: "Whittinghill! Whittinghill!"

Do you know how startling this is to hear your name called out in a foreign land where you don't know a soul?

"WHITTINGHILL!"

It turns out to be a regular listener from back home, Ed O'Shaugnessy, who has been playing tapes of my morning show for the customers at The Bailey. Later, one of the bartenders was to say, "So you're Whittinghill. I feel I know ya', since this fellow here has been playin' your program for a week!"

Settling down for our last dinner in beautiful Ireland, I order local trout with grapes and walnuts and scampi. But I start it off with something unusual that catches my eye immediately—fresh tomato soup with gin!

"You make this with real gin?" I ask the waiter.

"Oh, yes, sir."

"Well, bring it on."

The waiter brings this big tureen of lovely soup. He ladles it out for me and then takes a shaker, this little jug, and shakes it over my tomato soup.

"Hit me again," I said.

He shook some more in the soup—and several more shakes.

Let me tell you, it is delightful. And now every time I have tomato soup, I insist on a couple of shots of gin in it.

As we left Ireland and watched that wonderful green land fade far beneath us, I waved goodbye to the Old Sod—and its colorful golf courses, castles, Fergus, the goats, The Bailey, the fresh tomato soup, the fishless lakes, the quaint taverns, and most of all, Sneem.

I'll be back you darlin' people. Old Whit will be back.

3

Ski-Nose vs. the Great One

I WENT DOWN to Palm Springs early this year to join the frolicking surrounding the Bob Hope Desert Classic, one of pro golf's truly glamorous events, which annually attracts some of the biggest entertainers in the business along with some of the biggest spenders.

In other years, I played in the pro-am division but it makes me too nervous now, especially if I'm on television. I get the dry throat, my eye starts to twitch, and my knees knock, which produces a swing like a guy falling out of a revolving door. The way I go through life, why do I need to make a sap out of myself before a national television audience? I do that every day on the air but no one *sees* me.

We don't get to the Springs as often as we'd like, even though we have a little hovel there right across the street from Bob Hope's home. I've been renting it to this darlin' elderly couple for $350 a month—two bedrooms and a swimming pool, so no one can accuse me of being a gouging landlord. But

13

this nice couple takes good care of it and that's all I care about.

Before the start of the Desert Classic, I'm at Hope's big cocktail party, laughing and scratching and enjoying all the famous people there including former President Gerald Ford. And, of course, as always, the Kid from Montana is in awe of him, and all the others.

I'm sipping a little Crown Royal when Dolores Hope glides by and begins telling me what an awful problem she's having accommodating all of her relatives and close friends who want to attend the tournament.

"Whit," she says, "would you rent your home to me for the next three days for $1,000 a day?"

Well, I nearly dropped my glass and my other fist snapped shut so tightly I broke my Ritz cracker.

"Gee, Dolores, I'm sorry but I rent my place to this elderly couple for $350 a month," I said, with my voice trailing off weakly.

"You're kidding?" she gasped.

Just then President Ford's group is coming around again and I'm pleased to see that he's having a little shooter, too. And someone pulls me by the arm and says, "Mr. Ford, have you met Dick Whittinghill?"

And the former president of the United States says, "Oh, yes, I met this young man earlier tonight."

Young man! Why, I'm older than he is.

Pretty soon Hope comes over and whispers, "Whit, how would you like to follow Jackie and me around the course tomorrow. It's the annual Grudge Match." Bob Hope vs. Jackie Gleason.

I was delighted; of course I would. As it happened, Hope had not invited a large party this time; it had grown too large over the years. So here I am, the little disc jockey from Hollywood, privileged to follow two great comics around a beautiful golf course. The only other guest for the Grudge Match was a former councilman, Warren Dorn, of Los Angeles.

Now, Hope and Gleason bet big money on this match—thousands—the loser's end going to the winner's favorite charity. For Hope it's the Eisenhower Medical Center in Palm Springs and for Gleason it's Boys' Clubs in the Miami Beach area of Florida.

We're on the course riding around in a little cart with no gallery and you'd expect that there would be no jokes, right? Wrong. Suddenly Dorn and I become the gallery and Hope and Gleason are throwing one-liners at *us*.

In the middle of the match, Hope says, "The last time I beat a fat man, I beat Jackie Pung!" And Gleason snarls, shakes his head like Ralph Kramden accepting a zinger from Alice, and retorts, "Whittinghill, tell your radio listeners about Hope's new book—*How To Line Up Your Fourth Putt*."

Now they're acting like petulant school kids.

"Jackie, you teed that ball up! You can't do that. Summer rules. C'mon, Jackie!"

"I did not, Bob. I did not tee that ball up!"

"Tough luck. Ha, ha!" Hope says, after Jackie hooks one into the trees.

"Oh, look at that. Took off like a bird!" Jackie coos after hitting a nice straight drive.

"Whittinghill can hit it farther with his *cane*," Hope cracks.

"You were chipping better *without* your corset," Jackie needles.

It went on this way all afternoon. I never had so much fun watching a golf match.

The Grudge Match came out even and the thousands that were bet will be doubled up for the next time they meet in February of 1978. Two great guys doing a nice, never-publicized bit for charity. Truly, they are as big as their talents.

4

These Are *My* People

I WAS DELIGHTED and very surprised at the tremendous success of my first book, the legendary and fabled *Did You Whittinghill This Morning?* Don't you know it's part of my job to give the commercial? OK, end of commercial.

Sitting behind the microphone six days a week, one tends to forget who one's audience is. Unless you make a career out of attending supermarket openings, like I used to for sponsors, you occasionally have to be reminded that there are all kinds of people out there.

I found out, happily so, about my people when I was caught up in their mainstream during a number of autograph appearances for my first book at various department stores and bookstores in Southern California. Naturally, we were hustling my first epic with all the gusto we could muster.

My people were ready for me, bless their hearts. They're wonderful people of all ages, and I'm grateful to have them aboard. But as I said, they were *ready* for me.

One of our first stops was at Robinson's in the city of La Puente in fast-growing Orange County where the California Angels dwell. (I threw that in because my boss, Gene Autry, owns the baseball team: Is that two commercials?) I was shocked by the number of people waiting in line. They were jolly and I was jolly, but about two hours later I had writer's cramp and was looking for my driver to take me away.

Just as we got up to leave, a little old lady with white hair and a print dress and smiling eyes timidly approached me. "Will your book ever be in paperback?" she asked. "I can't afford the hardback."

"Well, I don't know . . ." I said. Then I looked into the eyes of this dear thing, who was beginning to back away, clutching her tiny purse.

I folded. Wilted. Got choked up. What else could I do? I bought her a copy of the book, autographed it, and she thanked me softly and stole away.

"She probably does this at all the stores," my driver said, destroying a touching moment in my literary life. He was only kidding, I think, and the little lady never showed up again at any of the many book stops along the trail.

In Anaheim one Saturday at noon, another long line was waiting for Dick *Hemingway*, author and sometimes disc jockey. I realized by then that the people were expecting a show, so I'd have several jokes rehearsed or some funny stuff about KMPC's freeway reporters, Panther Pierce and Dave DeSoto, or the latest golf joke handed down by the station's jet helicopter pilot, long John McElhenny. All of these characters provide information and wisecracks every morning on the program, and I soon found out that the fans wanted to hear all about my colorful colleagues.

The department stores set up places for authors, with desk, chair, and microphone, and everyone can hear everything the author and book-buyer say.

In Anaheim, the first lady in line is a very motherly type, with a big warm bosom. She clutches me and knocks my glasses off. "You ugly thing you!" she giggles. Then she stands back and holds my face in her hands, tweeks my cheeks, and knocks my glasses off again. I'm embarrassed and people are laughing. "Oh, you ugly thing you!"

In Arcadia, we had another festive bunch. But one sweet soul really broke up the place. She must have been in her early sixties and, not realizing a microphone was there, whispered, "Would you write down 'To one morning man from another'?" Then she giggled evilly. The whole line heard it and laughed.

And I said, "How *is* he in the morning?"

And she started giggling and scampered away.

In Lakewood, huge line. It was hot. But a thoughtful young woman brought me a big glass of water with ice. How nice. I took a big slug of it—glub, glub!—it was straight gin! She stood back laughing and I'm coughing and tears are running down my face.

Well, Old Loudmouth, you certainly asked for it. It's the role you play, pal.

5

Whittinghilling in Wax
(. . . a horror story)

REMEMBER HOW I FOUGHT my butt off to win that precious little boxing trophy from the University of Montana? You can search my living room and it's eight-to-five you won't find it. You can win bigger ones playing Skee Ball at the local penny arcade. I fought so hard for that dinky thing, and I didn't do a darn thing for my biggest material honor.

Let us go back to an evening a few years ago when I made a mistake and flew by Lakeside on the way home and accidentally ended up at home. The family looked at me like I was a cat burglar.

"Someone steal your golf clubs?" Wilamet needled.

"You're never home at this hour on *Thursday*," Nora said in mock amazement.

Just then a phone call came from Doug Anderson of the Chamber of Commerce. "Called Lakeside and they said you weren't there," Anderson said. "Didn't expect to find you home on *Thursday*." What is this *Thursday* bit? I thought. Is it evil to play golf on Thursday? Am I a local disgrace to my family and friends on Thursday?

We conversed for a few minutes and I hung up and the expression on my face was reflected on the faces of my family. They gave me the Pacoima stare.

"You'll never believe this," I said.

"Yes we will," said daughter Willy, like they would and do believe everything that happens to me.

"The Hollywood Chamber of Commerce wants to put me in the Wax Museum!"

"You mean like those wax figures in that French museum?" Nora asked.

"Yeah."

"That's a scream," said daughter Willy.

"What's so funny about it? No other deejay is in a wax museum. I think that's kind of important."

The girls giggled.

"What'll we *do* with it?" Wilamet wondered.

"We won't *do* anything with it. People will go and look at it."

"Why would anybody want to do *that*?" my darlin' wife said in all sincerity.

I posed for this wax sculptor (I forget his name) for a couple of hours one morning while he made sketches and measured my head and checked my height and weight. I felt stupid.

"You will love it," he said, like a true press agent.

As usual, KMPC and its fireball PR man, Warren Turnbull, got behind the project with the customary gusto of a good Hollywood promotion, and a grand press party was set for the unveiling, which was held at the Broadway Department Store on Hollywood and Vine. To my surprise a big crowd and a fine press turned out to see a loudmouth disc jockey immortalized in wax.

So, I'm in another room going over my little speech and belting down a few vodkas, getting my mouth in shape, and nibbling on some hors d'oeuvres when I feel a pop in my mouth. Oh, boy, a broken cap on my front tooth. I can't talk, the words only whistle and woosh out of my dumb mouth.

"Hold everything!" I whistled to a startled Warren Turnbull. "I'll be back as soon as I can!"

"What's wrong?" he stammered.

"Got to find a dentist!"

Warren's mouth was agape as I ran out of the Broadway and down the street, in and out of every big office building until I found a dentist.

Dashing into his suite, I commanded the receptionist to get me in right away; this was an emergency! The little old ladies and men waiting their turns to have their plates fixed looked up astonished at this crazed interloper with a tooth cap clutched in the palm of his hand.

I explained who I was and that a couple of hundred people were waiting for me to make a speech, and the assistant is thrilled because she listens to my program. She gets on the intercom, whispers in a low voice and this diminutive Japanese man (from USC as it turned out) appears in a white smock. "Come right in, Mr. Whittinghill, I listen to your show every morning."

This stock line never sounded so good as I plopped into the chair and handed him my broken-off cap. So he's chatting and drilling and I'm glancing at my watch and he says the magic words:

"Oh, oh!"

(My mind flashed back to the last time I heard this phrase in a critical situation, under circumstances I normally try to avoid: We were flying back from Hawaii and the whole family was nervous, especially my wife, who can fly 10,000 miles with her eyes shut. Me, I just have four or five shooters and never unlock my seat belt until I feel earth.

Well, we're cruising along in splendid weather and the captain gets on the PA system and he sounds real happy, giving the time, air speed, weather forecast, and then, abruptly— "Oh, oh!"

There's a deadly silence—and the plane starts down, fast, to about 15,000 feet above the glasslike Pacific Ocean. Seems the air pressure equalizer, or whatever they call it, had gone bugs, and was it getting hot! The stewardesses were darting up and down the aisle with cold cloths for the passengers' foreheads, and when one of them got to me I said, "Never mind the cold rag, get me a double Martini!" And she did, bless her.)

"Oh, oh!" the Japanese dentist said.

He had broken the stem of my capless tooth and there wasn't time to do the proper repairs, so he used an old American trick—a piece of gum—and stuck the cap on. It worked beautifully.

I dashed back to the Broadway where the press contingent hadn't noticed the time slipping by since Warren was busy funneling booze down their happy throats. But quickly, he brought them to attention and all eyes focused on the sheet-covered figure of Old Loudmouth.

I said a few words, thanked the Chamber and Doug Anderson (now of Anderson, McConnell and Oakner), put an arm around my beaming daughters, and pulled the string.

Willy and Nora screamed, covered their eyes, and turned away.

There *it* sat. I looked like a corpse with my best Lakeside sweater on and one of my most expensive pair of slacks. It was a startling thing. And, frankly, I didn't like it. Some of my press friends agreed, making critical comments behind their hands as they filed out. Later, my sculptor reworked *its* frozen puss and *it* looks slightly more like me now.

My waxen twin sat in the front of the Hollywood Wax Museum (Hollywood Boulevard near Highland Avenue in case you stumble by) for some time; *it* looked like I was taking tickets and I saw people going up and feeling and scratching my face, and this sort of annoyed me.

It has been moved back from the door since then, and now I'm staring across the room at Glen Campbell.

Neither one of us looks too thrilled by it.

6

My Daughter, the Poet

WHEN THEY WERE LITTLE they were as cute and inquisitive and mischievous as any of their playmates, and maybe more so. And, I always thought, more loving than any kids in the world.

We spent a lot of time sharing as they grew up—all of us, Wilamet, Willy, and Nora and Old Dad. We played and laughed and learned and shared. Somehow, Willy and Nora survived childhood and adolescence and became darlin', responsible adults. I shouldn't say *somehow* because they have the greatest mother in the world. And, OK, Dad was always there to listen and advise and love, even though the casual observer might think I spend all of my spare moments at Lakeside.

It was quite a number of years before I discovered I was harboring my own Emily Dickinson—daughter Willy. Willy has always been the quieter of the two, less demonstrative but at the same time the unofficial second in command of the domestic household. Even today, she runs a tight ship and finds time to work on the outside, too. Of course, her mother worries that she'll stay too long in the nest. But I don't want her to leave, either. You parents know how it is.

But here I go again, running off at the mouth. As I said, one day I found out that I had a poet in the family. It was on a Mother's Day not long ago. Willy gave (dedicated, presented?) a poem to her mother, and it was beautiful and I was so proud. It has no title, but it doesn't need one.

Daughter Willy's poem to her mother:

> The thanks and understanding
> For all the love she gave me
> A tribute to my life
> For everything she's done for me
> The tears she shed and always hid
> For her help and reassurance
> I could have been her friend
> But something wouldn't let me
> What was it deep inside
> That hid my deep affection
> The quiet that hid the thanks
> The pain that dried my tears
> Because of her I grew
> Reflected from her I glowed
> Loved by her I learned to love
> And although I never showed it
> Forever all this was taken for granted
> Your baby I was
> My mother you are
> A carbon of you and all of life
> With your love I've grown
> I admit it's hard to say
> Words much easier to write
> Know I love you, your work

> Believe I've always cared
> Because you are what made me.

Isn't that lovely? Would it mean more to you, the reader, to know that daughter Willy is adopted?

Maybe Willy will never have her poems published in a book of poetry, but this is *my* book and I'm going to see that some of them see the light here. Now, we've all been here for laughs in two books, so it's time for something wonderful and warm before we get back to the golf course and the shooters.

Here's more, and I don't mind telling you I don't always want to know the source or reason for such inspiration:

> I just can't seem to understand
> I can't put us together
> I tried so hard to care
> I guess I wanted too much
> But what is it that you mean
> What can't you tell me
> I see your little games
> You're in another league
> And I'm still sitting on the bench
> After all the tries and all the strikes
> All the lies and all the love
> Trying to make something
> Out of almost nothing
> I see everything I could have done
> i could have made it all more fun
> I thought I was too selfish
> But hurt I won't let touch me
> My lack of caring to protect me
> My future forever, the light too dim to see
> Don't let me hurt you
> I think we have changed places
> Perhaps I'll realize when the time is gone

I guess I'll care after you have left
And gone our love forever.

And another one:

> What if
> Through dreams and plans
> The reality of actually building
> Working toward a world
> A career, a business
> What if
> When all was finished
> No more long hours
> Nor hard work building
> What if
> Nothing happened.

This one touched me. How could she know?

> This day marks the beginning
> The joining of two into one
> The end of you and I
> And the start of us
> A tear falls down on Daddy's cheek
> Arm in arm he gives me away
> For now I'm only yours
> Everybody waits and watches
> The room filled with warmth
> The sunlight leads the way
> The love lights our path
> I do, I will, forever.

This is nice, too:

I
Can not
See the
Love
Shine
In your
Eyes
For it
Shines
From your
Heart
Making
Your whole
Face
Glow.

7

It's Not What I Said . . .

I WENT TO ACTING SCHOOL, REMEMBER? I was going to be the next Warren William. And I've been in a number of movies, musicals, and literally dozens of television shows. And how about appearing in the only picture Cagney ever directed?

Maybe I'm not a first-rate actor, but I perform well and always knew how to take direction. I was directed by taskmasters like Jack Webb and as I mentioned, Cagney. To me, learning lines is easy.

So along about the time I'm doing "Dragnet" for Webb, I get a call from the late Ozzie Nelson's producer asking me if I'd like to work in the "Ozzie and Harriet" series, and I said, "Splendid." It's not a tough show and it's in the top ten and it'll be fun and my family will love seeing the old man with Dave and Rick and all those popular television kids.

The script is sent to the house, which is customary. Looking it over, it's a nice little part with just enough dialogue to make it comfortable. And I was looking forward to working with

Ozzie, who was one of the nicest guys in the business and, of course, a fellow musician. Yes, it would be a jolly experience.

I knew my lines and was fully prepared when I met director Nelson on the set and we kibitzed about radio and sports and I met the Nelson family, all just as nice and friendly in person as they were on the tube.

Now we're in rehearsal and muttering our lines and finding our marks, etc. Now it's action time and actor Whittinghill picks up the telephone and utters his first line to Ozzie on the other end:

"I'll meet you at the airport at nine o'clock, okay?"

"CUT!" Ozzie yells.

"Dick," he says, "let's do it again, that's not quite right."

I look around, puzzled. I knew I had the line right.

"What did I leave out?"

"It's not quite right, Dick. Please, let's try it again . . . . Action!"

"I'll meet you at the airport at nine o'clock, okay?" I delivered the line with a little more emotion.

"CUT!"

My right cheek and eye start to twitch. What now?

"Dick, listen to the line as I read it," Ozzie said, pleasantly.

"I'll-meet-you-at-the-air-port-at-nine-o'clock, o-kay?"

To myself I say, that's exactly what I said, word for word. Maybe I'll give it less emotion.

"Action!"

"I'll meet you at the airport at nine o'clock, okay?"

"CUT!"

Ozzie smiles, I'm twitching. "Let's break for lunch and we'll pick up Dick's scene when we resume," he says. Everybody dashes for the commissary and I'm standing there repeating the line over and over and looking at my script. What the hell am I doing wrong? All during lunch, I'm going over the stupid line and I'm becoming more confused.

Ozzie's co-star, Lyle Talbot, a grand fellow, realizes what

I'm going through after eight takes and stops me on the way back to the set.

"Dick," he says, "I've worked with Ozzie a long time and he can destroy you, but if you don't let him, he's beautiful."

"How do you mean?"

"When we go back in there, do your line and he'll ask you to do it over. Do it over, but do it exactly the way he *says* it. I mean just exactly in his staccato delivery, copy it as precisely as you can. He has a beat, like a line of music. You'll see."

And Ozzie asked me to repeat it and I listened to him and I did it:

"I'll-meet-you-at-the-air-port-at-nine-o'clock, o-kay?"

"That was great, Dick."

"Thanks, Oz."

With my new style, I did about two more "Ozzie and Harriet" episodes.

8

Honest Dick, Used-Car Salesman

I'VE ALWAYS HAD a great relationship with sponsors. In fact, I have a habit of going overboard at times, and early in my days at KMPC I outsmarted myself with one particular client who had bought a large chunk of time on the Saturday morning program. Remember, you can sell me anything.

As a gimmick and good public relations for the client, whom we'll call Bud Murphy's Used Cars, we broadcast a remote from the parking roof of his Hollywood agency.

We had a standard routine. Between records I'd pop in with old Bud and describe a car and give the price and, naturally, when a listener-customer rushed down to buy it, it was already sold. I was too naive and too busy with all of the mechanics of doing a four-hour radio program to understand or worry about how these early car slickers operated.

So there I was on the sunny roof with Bud and Stanley L. Spero, then a promising salesman (now vice president and general manager of the station, as you've learned from previous accounts, I hope).

37

Between records, the drivers would zoom up in these cars and come to a screeching stop for good radio sound effects. One driver, obviously stoned out of his mind, went right by me and slammed into another car. I broke up but cleverly hid it while a record was on. Undaunted, I gave my pitch:

"Here folks, we have a neat 1955 Olds, dark green, all the extras including a radio, and low mileage . . ." And so on.

In the background came another sound, also good for radio sound effects.

HONK! HONK! SCREECH! HONK! HONK!

"Get that pile of junk out of my way!" yelled a driver.

We immediately went to a record.

"Well, folks, it's good Old Whit back again with another fine used car buy from Bud Murphy." And then they wheeled up a dandy-looking, near new Buick.

So I gave the pitch: "a beautiful blue Buick . . ." and I named an outrageous price, but I wasn't listening to myself because I really liked the car. "You know, folks, *I'm* so crazy about this Buick that *I'm* going to buy it!"

Murphy is waving his arms frantically and whispering, "No, no, no!" but I'm oblivious to his warnings, not knowing at the time that because it was advertised on radio, he had to sell it to me at that price.

"Yessir, I'm going to buy this Buick, but if you want a good value like this one, get right down to Bud Murphy's Used Car Lot."

Old honest Dick bought the outrageously priced car for an outrageous price and, as a matter of fact, I made two trips to Montana in it.

Which reminds me of the nicest little car I ever had, which I won in some sponsor's promotion. It was a 1910 Oldsmobile, cute as a little bug with spiffy black leather upholstery and one of those ahhh-oooogah horns. We had lots of fun in it, spinning around the neighborhood waving at our friends and tooting the horn. We were becoming a local attraction in the antique machine. I even wore a big white touring hat and goggles on occasion.

But, of course, I had to screw it up as usual.

One day I'm tooling around the block in it and I've had a few belts and I spot Jim Healy, the demon sportscaster, pulling into his driveway. As it turned out, Jim had had a few belts, too.

"Get in Jimbo, let's take a ride!" I yell.

Off we go, careening around like those cars in the Keystone Kops comedies. Well, this 1910 Olds didn't have a steering wheel, but it had a tiller, or long handle, which operated the opposite way the car was going. In other words, to turn left, you turned the tiller to the right.

We're breezing along, laughing and waving to the neighbors, when I paused to light a cigarette. "Take the tiller, Jim," I said, not thinking that he possibly hadn't tilled a tiller before. But he tilled, and we crashed right into the curb, like a scene from Laurel and Hardy. My dark glasses flew off and Healy was pitched forward onto a lawn. There was a pause, then a loud BANG! And the Olds was dead. Healy lurched to his feet and I staggered out of the machine as smoke curled from its engine. There we were, two half-loaded nuts looking blankly at each other and then falling into fits of laughter.

I managed to salvage the dear old thing, and I sold it to actress June Lockhart. I think she eventually made a planter out of it.

9

The Vikings of Scandia
(. . . my kind of guys)

SCANDIA IS A WORLD-FAMOUS RESTAURANT on the Sunset Strip. It is expensive and worth it. It is demanding—gentlemen wear coats—and deserves it. It takes weeks to get a weekend reservation, and it's worth the wait. The bar (one of the town's handsomest), however, doesn't accept reservations and the door is always open.

It's nice to have a Scandia in a time and town where everybody is so casual you're likely to see guys wearing blue jeans to the Music Center or girls wearing bikinis to the race track. Class is an endangered species.

Ken Hansen founded the restaurant many years ago and it soon became a meeting place for a lot of Hollywood celebrities. I danced in sometime in the early fifties and immediately blended in with the decor and the laughing beverages. We became a close group, which included several Lakesiders. By the time Hansen outgrew his modest surroundings the place had become famous.

So Hansen moved up the boulevard to the edge of Beverly Hills and Johnny Weissmuller, the funny, gregarious Tarzan of the movies, and Dick Whittinghill, radio's designated loudmouth, led the parade on white horses down Sunset to Scandia's new and present location. And there it sits, elegantly, through all these years of change. The hippies are gone and so is the exotic burlesque house or strip joint across the street. Scandia remains. All hail Scandia!

Scandia also is the name of the Vikings, the most charitable group in the world. The Vikings are not restricted to one occupation and its members come from all walks of life and all levels of society. But many sports stars, politicians, lawyers, doctors, and entertainers are members. I mean, big names. I've always felt honored to find my name on the list of Viking members. There it is, *Whittinghill*, last on a list that includes federal judges, novelists, Academy Award-winners, and Willie Mays.

We meet on the last Monday of every month to get a little smashed and have lunch. Sometimes we don't get to the lunch part, heh, heh. The main purpose, though, make no mistake about it, is charity for children. Any children's organization. In fact, you cannot belong to the Vikings unless you do one of two things—give blood twice a year or make Christmas baskets. I'll tell you about this part of it in a moment.

When I was chief of the Vikings, some time ago, at the end of the year we split up sixty or seventy thousand dollars for various charities, from a modest group of generous people. And may I boast that the Vikings have the biggest blood bank in the country outside of the Red Cross.

You have the picture, now. We're not exactly the town's only floating gin mill as some people might think who don't understand the cause. Actually, I like to think we've combined the best features of being sociable and charitable.

So let me here relate some of the funny and serious moments in Viking lore. Have a grog and we'll proceed.

When I was chief of the Vikings, I received a call from Father Garrett who ran a school for youngsters in the San Fernando Valley. The good father inquired about our expanding activities and told me of the school's desperate need for money and an automobile.

Well, I figured, here's this kindly father out there in the orange groves and the hot weather and his poor kids were stuck without a car. I could envision people bringing in donations of food and clothing. A father should have a car to run to the market in and take kids to the ball game.

I wanted peace in the Valley, so I put my wife's car, which was all paid for, up for auction under the auspices of the Vikings. We auctioned it off, got the money for it, then gave the car *and* the money to Father Garrett! I was proud and the Vikings were indeed happy about it.

Then Father Garrett came up to accept the car. It was then I found out he was Protestant! I thought he was a Catholic priest all this time. Let me tell you, it was touch and go whether or not I'd let him have the keys.

We do a lot for the MS (multiple sclerosis) kids. MS is really tragic. Some of the children can't move and they're in wheelchairs. It breaks your heart, but doing things for them gladdens your heart.

The Vikings take a group of them fishing each year down at the pier in Santa Monica. You never saw such joy on a child's face, even for those whose fishing poles have to be held for them. We want each child to catch fish, so a few of us roll up our trousers and wade into the water under the pier and put fish we've purchased in markets on the kids' hooks, and they reel them in. You've never seen such joyful expressions in your life.

Also once a year, we have a big luncheon for the kids and cook for them, you know, hamburgers and fries, and distribute all kinds of prizes.

The blood bank is a huge function and, as I said, everybody gives blood or participates in the children's Christmas ritual. The blood-giving day is quite an occasion; practically everybody shows up.

In the past we also invited the ladies to blood bank day, but we've had to exclude them. Inexplicably, they'd come out and just get drunk and the fellows who brought them would get drunk, too, and forget to give blood. So we had to throw the girls out.

And, yes, you can drink a little and give blood. Somehow, it has no effect. But I always say those who got my blood have to be the happiest recipients in the world.

Those who give blood also share in the Christmas basket day, along with the guys who faint at the sight of needles and blood, yes, especially their own.

When the Vikings first started making Christmas baskets it was done in a more or less loose fashion. We'd line up at 6:30 in the morning, our little boney knees knocking in the cold, and throw stuff in the baskets and load them into cars. I remember my first Christmas delivering them.

I was swelling with Christmas spirit, warmed by an eggnog or two, as I toddled up the stairs of this poor wretched family's apartment somewhere in Los Angeles. I could hear the little children fighting with one another as I prepared to knock. This will light the lamp of their Christmas dreams, I thought.

Knock, knock, knock!

"Yeah?" said the gentleman answering the door. He was tough looking. Unshaven. Soiled undershirt.

"Merry Christmas, sir!" I pushed the basket of toys and food and nuts into his hairy arms.

"What's this?" he barked.

"Why, sir, it's for your family—Merry Christmas!"

"Who is it, honey?" twanged a female voice from the inner darkness, as the kids continued fighting.

"Oh, it's some joker with a basket of fruit!" he yelled over his shoulder. "You from some charity?" he asked.

"Well, no, well, sort of . . . it's for your family. . . ."

"Get lost, buster! We don't take no charity!"

He advanced on me threateningly, and I nearly fell down the stairs trying not to spill my Christmas basket while three-stepping it to the street.

SLAM!

The kids were still fighting as I drove back to Scandia.

Since that first disaster, we now have a list of needy families provided by charitable organizations, and the rewards of beaming children and mothers and fathers are a blessing, making it a joy for all of us.

Initiation into the Vikings is joyful, too. In fact, it's downright hysterical. We wear the helmets with the Viking horns and little bibs. Let me tell you about the time we initiated the distinguished actor, Jack Lemmon.

We have a ritual of secrecy and we recite stuff; a bunch of grown men acting like kids, dressed in all this nonsense with robes on.

And we pause in the ceremony and say, "OK, fledglings, drink!" And these new members have to drink this huge bowl of a concoction of wine, beer, vodka, and whatever. They have to throw it down. Then our steward, Lud Veigel, who happens to be the town's highest paid bartender, throws his empty glass into this flaming bucket and we all throw our glasses in the bucket. Then we go to lunch. That's it.

So we initiate Lemmon and he drinks the concoction and throws his glass into the flaming bucket and we go to lunch and have some more shooters. Lemmon is a very entertaining fellow and we're certainly enjoying his company, but now it's getting late and he has to go.

As we later found out, Jack was sailing along Sunset Boulevard heading for Beverly Hills when he gets stopped by the police.

One of the officers asked him if he had been drinking?

Lemmon said that he only had a couple with lunch.

Here's the tableau:

Lemmon is telling two policemen he only had a couple of drinks with lunch, and he's sitting in his car with a Viking helmet with horns—and a bib on.

10

Who Needs an Idiot Card?
(... one guess will do)

ALMOST THREE DECADES AGO, this jolly fellow was commissioned to do his first television commercial. Live. In front of a camera.

Of course, I was a bit nervous. Everyone is the first time he appears before a camera. But I had started out to be an actor long ago and had many movies to my credit, along with network radio and my daily program. So what is that tough about doing a simple 60-second commercial for local audiences?

So I'm going to do a live commercial on Channel 13, which was KLAC-TV in those days—"Lucky Channel 13." I don't remember what product was involved, but I do remember that I had a prop, a piece of gold ore, that I was to hold up and say, "This is a piece of ore . . ."

I always could remember my lines, but I wanted to be perfect in this live spot, so I rehearsed for what seemed like hours with Willy as my sole audience. I rehearsed and rehearsed until Willy was beginning to know it better than I did. Finally, I felt I had it. And by now Willy had had it. So I toddled off to Channel 13.

KLAC-TV was a cheerful place in those days right in the heart of Hollywood. It was stucco and brick and covered with Spanish tile and had a huge patio in its center where the early talk show host, Tom Duggan, formerly did his live show. I observed immediately that the atmosphere was very casual. Most of TV was freewheeling in those days. It was fun.

I went to the assigned stage. I looked around for the floor manager. No floor manager. I looked for the director. No director. In fact, no one was there. By now it was 10 minutes before the indicated break in the movie and my commercial. I was sort of walking in circles looking for the glass control booth when a voice came out of the darkness.

"You got five minutes," it said. "When the red light goes on, you go on."

"Sir! Sir!" I called out. No answer. I wanted someone to hold my hand. There were no idiot cards to read from. "Sir!"

Then I noticed a camera being pushed toward me, but I couldn't make out if anyone was operating it. Of course someone was. Cameras don't move by themselves. The big studio clock on the wall said 30 seconds to go until the movie break. Glancing at the monitor, I could see cowboys chasing Indians, or was it Indians chasing cowboys?

Suddenly, a little red light went on, and the camera came in for a close-up. (I had found my mark on the floor and snatched the piece of gold ore from a nearby table.)

"Th-this is a piece of o-ore," I began. Then I went completely blank. It seemed like five minutes went by, me staring at that camera holding up that piece of ore. The red light was still on. The camera didn't move.

I put down the ore on the table and walked out of the studio, got into my car, and drove home. I never went back. Never found out what happened.

"Gee, I'm sorry, honey, I got busy with dinner and forgot about your commercial," Willy said. "I missed it."

"I know," I said.

11

My Television Career
(. . . from soup to nuts)

SEVERAL YEARS after I blew the live TV commercial, things began to pick up for the Kid from Montana. In the fifties television was continually experimenting with various live shows and new game and audience participation programs.

Since television was new, a lot of local stations were using radio announcers as hosts and evidently the TV people liked my morning show and they regarded me as "hot" host material.

So I wound up hosting movies for two television stations—Channel 4 and Channel 11.

I'd do the radio program, dash home and take a quick nap, then rush over to Channel 11 for its afternoon movie, then run home and have dinner, and then scurry back to Hollywood for Channel 4's early-evening movie. I was doing three shows a day.

Earlier, I was hosting one film a day on Channel 4 and the late Mike Roy, also a radio veteran, was hosting a morning cooking show. Things being as loose as they were in those days, occasionally we'd switch. I'd host his cooking show and he'd host my movie.

There wasn't much to do on the cooking show; Mike would have a guest cook there and I would look over his shoulder and smack my lips, inhale the exotic sauces and soufflés and say, "Yum, yum." The only real work was doing, yes, a live commercial or two. But by now I didn't blank out, so there were no "this is a piece of ore" problems.

One day I'm subbing for Mike Roy and I introduce a new product, a really good barbecue sauce called Chris & Pits, still very popular. Well, I sail into this commercial, holding up the bottle of sauce, and saying it's the greatest barbecue sauce in the world. Only I mispronounce the name. I call it Piss & Crits! But I thought I said it right, and I couldn't understand why the crew was falling over themselves laughing. Well, I made three more runs at it, every time calling it Piss & Crits.

Such was the gaiety of early live television.

Most of the people who had special shows had special sets, too. You know, tables, chairs, sofas, lamps, etc. I noticed some of the daytime hosts got new sets each week. So I thought it would be nice if I had a new set, too.

To my surprise they said sure. My first new set was some furniture from an outfit in Glendale, which we will call Fred Jones Furniture. It was arranged, like the other shows, that Fred Jones would get a plug every day for the use of his furniture. His name was on a big card and you always saw Fred Jones Furniture whenever I was on camera live with a guest.

At the end of the week I expected a new set and I told someone to send Fred Jones's furniture back to the store. I was told, "Oh, no, you take it home."

Take it home? It turns out this was the practice. Guys all over TV-land were furnishing their homes with the sets from their sponsors. And executives were getting new furniture for their offices.

I took the first set home but stopped the practice after that. To me, it was sort of like stealing. It just wasn't nice.

You may recall the big flap later in TV history when comics and hosts had to stop mentioning certain products because they were loading up on all sorts of expensive items and products.

A famous incident, when the practice was at its height, was some dialogue on Jack Benny's program. Rochester says something to Benny about preparing food and mentions something about using the Mixmaster. Benny says, "We don't have a Mixmaster." And Rochester says, "You do now!" It was an inside joke in those days.

Doing movies on Channels 4 and 11 was fun. But it presented problems filling time. Some days the director would say that I had 42 minutes of live time to fill. Well, you can't just talk for 42 minutes, even with commercials, so we had to improvise and think up nutty things to do.

The crews were great and they did inventive, spectacular camera things for me. For example, I'd start showing up in certain scenes of the movies. We had such terrible old films that these stunts actually improved them. But I'd never know quite what was happening, because I'd be in a basement room with blank walls, sitting on a chair covered with a white sheet or something and they'd superimpose me into a western gunfight scene, or I might surface in the middle of a lake while a couple was making love in a rowboat. Crazy stuff. But those great cameramen made it work perfectly.

The crews and I got to where we'd be pulling stunts on each other and, of course, the viewers loved it because it was so insane. One time, wondering how I was going to fill seven minutes at the end of the show, I simply motioned to the cameraman to follow me, and I walked out of the studio across the parking lot about 200 yards to a flight of stairs leading up to a door. What was behind it, I didn't know. But the camera recorded the whole scene. I went up the stairs, opened the door, and disappeared behind it.

And the camera focused on the closed door until time ran out. Remember, it was the Golden Age of Television. "Omnibus," "Your Show of Shows," "Playhouse 90," and the "Whittinghill Movie."

On other occasions the crew would pile debris up against the door as I prepared to make my exit. I had a standard close, with my radio theme song, "I'm Walkin' Out the Door," as sung by Nat Cole. Many times the crew piled so much stuff in front of the door I could hardly get out of the place.

Channel 4 was trying to find a vehicle for me in those times. *Vehicle* is television parlance for, "Find something this guy can do." It had me doing an evening show with Ginger Drysdale, wife of the great former ball player who now broadcasts games for the California Angels. Somehow, the brass thought that putting me on the air with a tall girl in shorts was funny. And while we were interviewing people and showing some film—I don't remember all the stuff we conjured up—guys would walk through the set, come in and out of doors, and we would ignore them. This was supposed to be funny. I made a fool of myself on that show. No one could find my *vehicle*. Mercifully, it was cancelled before many folks found out we were on the air.

All good (or bad) things must come to an end, as they say in the biz. And with Old Loudmouth, television came to an end without fanfare. My salad daze as Channel 11's "hot" movie host came to an end on the first night of a vacation with Willy in Las Vegas. Imagine, Channel 11 called me at the hotel in Vegas to inform me my services were no longer required.

It didn't stop Whittinghill, the thespian, however. I still turn up occasionally in shows like "Switch" and "Emergency." But these days I'm big playing newscasters and shoe clerks.

The way television is today, I think it's ready for another movie host doing crazy stuff. Maybe I can do a matinee live from the bar at Lakeside, starring Forrest Tucker, Don Knotts, Dennis James, George Gobel, Foster Brooks, Jim Murray, Mickey Rooney, and all the gang. What typecasting for your favorite little disc jockey!

I think I'll call my agent! What a vehicle!

12

How to Stop Smoking
(when the smoke clears)

I DON'T SMOKE ANYMORE, even though I've *tried* to start again twice in the last eight years.

The first time I tried to start again I couldn't stop gagging and coughing, but after two weeks of giving it all I had I was smoking again like a champ.

Unfortunately, I enjoy it. I'm ashamed to admit it, too. Once in a while I'll take just one drag from a friend's cigarette, feel my head spin, my eyes water and burn, my chest knot-up, and my throat go dry. Then I'll dab my eyes, smile, and go for another three or four months before taking another drag. That one jolt seems to do it. How suave.

Fortunately, the last time I tried to start up on a daily basis, it didn't work. I was wheezing and hacking too much, so I quit for good. Disc jockeys and practically everybody in the entertainment business smoke excessively. I guess it's because they have to keep operating or they get nervous and restless. Who better than Old Loudmouth understands that?

The subject of smoking reminds me of another typical screw-up of mine in the early fifties when I was trying to become a big hit in local television.

We were doing a 60-minute show at KHJ-TV, Channel 9, and I was doing everything—singing, dancing, telling jokes, playing the trumpet—all before a live audience.

So one day I'm standing in the wings waiting to go on and I light a cigarette. I take a couple of quick puffs and start to put it out when I feel a hand on my shoulder.

"See the sign, pal?"

It's the fire marshal.

"Well, no, I'm sorry, I didn't."

"There are No Smoking signs all over the studio," he says firmly.

"OK, I'll watch it next time. Excuse me, I've got to go on right now."

"I got to give you a ticket."

"Ticket? Can't you wait . . . I'm on, now. . . ."

So I dash onto the stage and I'm dancing and singing and telling these dumb jokes and it lasts quite awhile, and I come off perspiring and beat. And the fireman is waiting with my ticket. And I find out I have to go to court.

In Judge Clifton's court in downtown Los Angeles, I'm sitting around with strange-looking women and men, and two or three in front of me are appearing before the judge on charges of burglary, prostitution, and armed robbery, etc. One guy is even there for rape! I'm in with hardened criminals! For smoking!

There's a brief recess and we're all back in this room having a smoke and I overhear these very upsetting conversations:

"Man, this is my third rap . . . I don't know what's going to happen . . . ." "I'm a two-time loser, too . . ." "Got caught on a silent-ringer, didn't think that old store had one . . ." "You know, I been arrested by this stinkin' vice cop twice in the *same* apartment. He was wearin' a beard last time."

I'm nervous enough, but then one of them looks over at me, sizes me up (my spine begins rolling up like a window shade), and says, "What you in for, buddy?"

My mind starts clicking like a computer. I can't say I'm here for smoking ... These guys are bad ... I want to get along with them ... I haven't been working in "Perry Mason" all this time for nothing!

"I'm in here for a loft job," I said, sort of like Jimmy Cagney.

They seemed to look at me rather admiringly.

The bailiff calls us back and in a few minutes I'm catching on that someone (I can think of dozens of funsters who would have pitched in) apparently has tipped Judge Clifton that I'm Whittinghill, the morning man on KMPC, because now he's got me up there in front of the bench making light of my smoking violation and tee-heeing and I'm stammering and saying, "Well, your honor, I didn't see the No Smoking sign."

Judge Clifton is still kidding around with me and my ears start burning. I know all these burglars and rapists and robbers—the real pros—are back of me listening and finding out that I'm a fraud. That I'm just a disc jockey!

When jovial Judge Clifton tee-heed again and dismissed me, I walked up the aisle past these criminals as fast as I could. Out of the corner of my eye I could see the old prostitute looking up at me. She had a look of contempt.

A loft job.

It was embarrassing.

13

The Mountie and Yukon Lil

THIS IS ANOTHER "I Never Learn" episode, and I have to begin by going back to my college days.

In the Sigma Chi house, I met a rich kid from Detroit who owned a beautiful, long convertible, which dazzled my Kid-from-Montana eyes. What a smash I'd be if I could drive my friends around in that swell car, I thought. And I thought some more and came up with a nifty plan—I *thought*.

My dad, the executive with the Telephone Company, had a private line with his own coded number, and no matter who he called or where, Dad never got a bill.

"Listen," I said to my rich pal, "I'll let you use my dad's coded number and you can call anywhere if you'll let me drive your car now and then."

"Deal!" he said.

Naturally, it got out of hand. Not only did my wealthy compadre abuse the long-distance lines, but yours truly joined in too. And you already know I'm one of the original loud-mouths. Well, we called the pope in Rome (fortunately we never got through), the president in Washington, D.C. (but he was busy with the Depression), the emperor of Japan (Hirohito wasn't taking any calls, just buying scrap iron), and Duke Ellington in Harlem. The Duke was unavailable, but we did persuade the hatcheck girl to put his guitar player on the phone between sets.

Pretty soon, *I* got a call—from the vice president of the local telephone company. An appointment was arranged.

The vice president told me to sit down in his nice big office, but he stood up behind his desk waving a paper as his face reddened.

"This bill here is for $317, and your father says he didn't make these calls and says there isn't a chance in hell that *he* is going to pay it, and, I'll tell you something else, kid, neither is the Telephone Company!"

"I'm going to pay it?" I asked, weakly.

"That's the message, kid."

So, I got my trumpet out, put on a bow tie, and booked myself into the Park Hotel in Missoula—a flea bag. It was so rundown, "room service" was a bottle of creosote. It was so old, the hotel call girl didn't have a phone.

But I played there every night, nine to one in the morning, until that bill was paid off and my dad was talking to me again. Boy, did that teach me a lesson? Of course not.

Twenty years later at Lakeside, the Kid from Montana reinstated his telephone game. I'd line guys up at the bar after a noseful of shooters and we'd call weird sounding towns all over the United States and Canada, talking to anyone who'd listen and engaging in preposterous conversations until we fell down laughing.

One of our first calls was to exotic Athole, Idaho, where we got ahold of the county recorder and simply inquired how one pronounced the name of his town. It is pronounced exactly as it looks and when we asked him how it is spelled, he strangely slammed down the receiver to the howls of the hooched-up assemblage.

On another occasion, I really did a number on lovable Bob Beban, Lakeside's resident Martini-drinking champion. Pretending to be a deputy sheriff in Los Angeles, I phoned the chief of police of Intercourse, Pennsylvania. Today Intercourse is one place where Beban can't even *stop* for a drink. I told the chief of police to be on the lookout for Robert Beban, a local sex offender who was on the lam and expected to contact his relatives in Intercourse.

Beban was going nuts while the rest of the gang nearly choked with laughter. Beban, the *sex* offender, hiding in *Intercourse*! Aren't we subtle?

Our telephonic triumph, however, was a long series of calls to Moosejaw, Saskatchewan, Canada, where we made great friends with one of the Royal Canadian Mounted Police's finest, Sergeant Travis P. Witherspoon. He even sounded like Nelson Eddy. Witherspoon was the honcho and jailer in scenic Moosejaw, and he was so cooperative and nice that we became more interested in talking with him than putting him on.

During the first call, Sergeant Witherspoon told us about the humble town and when we asked about the weather, he said, "Just a minute." And you could hear him tramping across the jailhouse floor, creek, creek, creek. And then back again. "Snowin' like hell," he said. His delivery was sort of like George Gobel's, and the boys at the bar crumpled in hysterics.

"You got anybody in the slammer?" one of us asked.

"Just an old prostitute," the sergeant answered.

(An old joke suddenly flashed through my mind: You know what they call a Canadian five-cent piece? A nickel. No, Yukon Lil.)

"You mean you want to talk to her?" Witherspoon drawled. "Welllll, it is against the rules, but since you're callin' from Hollywood, I guess it's okay."

More sounds of feet trodding across the floor, more laughter at our end. Then the sounds of iron clanking, and the sounds of two pairs of feet, one pair heavy, the other pair clicking and quick like high heels. More laughter at our end.

From this point on, we'll call the old prostitute "Lil" after my joke.

After a brief exchange, Lil, still puzzled, said, "You guys movie stars down there?" And we say yes and put on one of our members who does a sensational impression of John Wayne.

"My favert pitture is 'She Wore a Yeller Ribbon'," Lil announces in reverent tones. We're holding our sides. And pretty soon, they're making a date whenever she's in Hollywood. Now we are roaring. What a sophisticated bunch we are. So suave. So intellectual.

Then Sergeant Witherspoon says, "Time is up" and Lil says, "Good-bye fellers, and I'll try to get down there as fast as I can, *Johnny*." And Yukon Lil went back to her slam pad.

Another time we call the sergeant and he's out tracking down a thief and the jailhouse gives us the number of the two-way radio in Witherspoon's jeep, and this is when we invited him to Hollywood. Right then, out of the middle of a snowstorm, he accepts, and one week later this true-blue mountie is getting off the plane at Los Angeles International Airport. I had arranged for him to visit Parker Center as a guest of the Los Angeles Police Department. Even Jack Webb agreed to have lunch with the now famous Mountie Witherspoon.

He and his wife stayed the weekend. And you know what he wanted to do? Visit Disneyland, for crying out loud. And that's *all* he did.

We haven't called Moosejaw lately, and Yukon Lil never showed up, either.

14

Three on the Rocks

EVERY MEN'S CLUB has its Peck's Bad Boys and Lakeside was once graced by three of the wildest, craziest guys of all. They bumped into more doors than the Three Stooges and downed more of the bubbly than the Three Musketeers.

The first sword of this group, its d'Artagnan, would be Bob Beban, the club's martini-drinking champion, who says he's going to be the first man in history to have a successful liver by-pass operation.

I never ran with these guys because I go home at night, but I occasionally accompany Beban to the racetrack or a Rams' game, and I'm always ready to play 18 with him. He's a splendid fellow, and funny.

Beban has fortunately outlived the original members of the cast, who were actor Grant Withers and a fellow named Trem Carr. And no one really qualifies at taking their places as the town's social gadabouts. Few can drink like them, either. Fewer could drink *with* them.

Anyway, Beeb joined me for lunch the other day and we're laughing and telling stories and having a jolly time. Then Beeb recalls his two favorite (and mine too) tales of the Tilting Trio. Let's run the tape back and hear Bob Begay tell it:

> It was the week between Christmas and New Year's—perhaps the worst time of the year other than St. Patrick's Day for imbibing around here—and myself, Mr. Withers, and Mr. Carr were in the cardroom when someone observed it was getting late and some of us had parties to go to.
>
> Withers and Carr began arguing over who was going to drive the car to Grant's house, which was only three blocks away. Finally, Trem drew himself up, emptied his scotch, and announced, "It's my car and I'm going to drive it!"
>
> We lurched out of the club, piled into Trem's automobile, edged out of the parking lot, and managed to negotiate the immediate danger, the corner of the lake (Toluca Lake). Moving slowly down Valley Spring Lane, which borders the back nine of Lakeside, I noticed a stop sign ahead with a car stopping in front of us. Trem didn't.
>
> CRUNNNNCCCCHHH!
>
> It wasn't much of a dent but it was a new car. Carr lurched out of his car and went up to the other driver and poked two $100 bills through the window, apologizing profusely and suggesting that $200 would more than cover the damages.
>
> So the other driver comes flopping out of his car and he is more stoned than any of us is.
>
> "This is bribery! You're not going to get away with this! I know the chiefapolice . . . my shun's an attor-ney!"
>
> He then fishes for an envelope and a pencil from his pocket and carefully leans over the hood and very carefully copies down his *own* license number.
>
> "My lawyers will contact you in the morning!"
>
> He fell into his car and disappeared into the night.

Now story number two, which is my favorite horserace story, and one, incidentally, I would have been a party to but at the last minute declined an invitation to join the Terrifying Threesome. Play it again, Beban:

We were on our way to Santa Anita Park for an afternoon at the races, and decided to meet at the Sheraton Town House for drinks. We went over the entries, made a preliminary choice in each race, and started out.

Just as we're passing a room where the hotel help have their lunch, a voice cries out: "Oh, gentlemen, Mr. Carr! Are you by any chance going to the track? You are? Wonderful. Will you then please bet this two dollars on Faithful Maude for me."

The voice belonged to the elevator operator, a little gal named Maude.

As we started out again, Maude had another inspiration. "If Faithful Maude wins," she says, "put it all on Deviled Egg in the third."

"Why Deviled Egg?" I ask.

"Because that's what I'm having for lunch," she says, a little of it dribbling from the corner of her mouth.

At the bar in the Turf Club, we all tried a way to justify betting on Faithful Maude. We couldn't. The horse was a bum. So the second race goes off and so does Faithful Maude. It wins and pays $156.40! So now Maude the elevator operator has won big and we're kicking each other for not even playing it as a hunch.

The next race is the Deviled Egg race and I notice that the odds on this sloth are 99-1, which means it could be anything because the tote board only shows 99-1 since there's only room for two numbers.

"We can't bet all this girl's money on this horse, it's ridiculous," says Mr. Carr. "This thing hasn't been in the money in two years!"

"We better do it," I said, "you know what happened to Faithful Maude."

"Bet $150 and keep the $6.40," Withers suggested, "and no matter what happens, she's got a profit."

It was agreed.

The race goes off and Deviled Egg is dead last. The horse is gray, so you can't miss it. They reach the half-mile post and Deviled Egg suddenly takes off like he was goosed with a red-hot poker. Right, he wins going away by two lengths, and Maude, the elevator operator, has won $14,000! That's *fourteen thousand dollars!* For *two bucks.*

Well, the word spreads throughout the Turf Club and now we have about 20 guys following us back to the Town House to watch the payoff. We all come in with Trem in the lead and he is waving *one* $100 bill, the rest bulging in his pocket.

"Hi, Mr. Carr, did I win?"

"Honey, you did."

Trem laid a $100 bill on her.

"All *this*?" she gasped.

"Yes, honey," Trem said, "and this, and this, and this . . ."

Trem proceeds to pile one hundred forty-four $100 bills on poor (until now), startled Maude. The color drains from her face and her little hands tremble as she stuffs all this money into her handbag. She didn't say a damn thing. She snapped her purse shut, got up from her little stool, and slowly walked over to the hotel manager standing at the desk.

"Mr. Groves," she said, "you can take your elevator and shove it up your ass."

And that's the last we ever saw of Maude.

15

The Art of Taking a Dive

IT WAS A FEW DAYS after Bing Crosby took that serious fall
on a Pasadena stage—after taping a television show commem-
orating his 50 years in show business—when I happened to
be having a late afternoon beverage with singer Mac Davis and
America's host, Dennis James.

"Gee, that was too bad about Bing," Dennis says.

"Really is," Mac adds, "and he's supposed to tape a TV
special with me in two weeks. Beautiful guy. He called from
the hospital last night and told me he is still planning to make
it."

"I took a fall off a stage once . . ." I started to say.

"I had a 240-pound wrestler fall on me once," Dennis says,
butting in. "Name was Tarzan Hewitt. I was calling the wres-
tling matches on TV back in New York, and I kidded old Tarz,
who was pretty fat, by saying, 'Look at the suet on Hewitt.'
Well, this made Tarzan mad when he heard about it, so the
next time he wrestled he threw his opponent out of the ring and
he landed in my lap."

Everyone was chuckling.

"I took a fall off a stage once . . ."

"I fell off a stage twice in the same night," Mac laughed. "It was a charity show down South and I got so carried away I fell off the side of the stage. Then, after another number, I got so carried away with the standing ovation, plus the cause, that I took a bow, threw open my arms and fell forward into the orchestra pit—on both knees!"

"Owwwwwwww," we all groaned in unison.

Bob Beban, overhearing the conversation, says, "You won't believe this, but I fell down in Colonel Sanders' last night!"

This, we believed.

"I should have called Bing," I said, "and asked him why he was stealing *my* routine. That's *my* routine."

The group seemed interested, so I continued.

"My fall was at the Forum (where the Los Angeles Lakers and Kings play) in front of 15,000 people! We were doing KMPC's Show of the World, and all the disc jockeys were there to introduce various stars. My bit was to introduce Bob Newhart.

"So I'm talking with Bob backstage and I say, 'Bob, here's what I'll do for a little gag. I'll introduce you by saying you're the funniest man I know and that all you have to say is "good evening" and I fall down. So you come up and say "good evening" and I'll fall down in front of the microphone.'

"Bob agreed and we went to our separate dressing rooms. Meanwhile, the show's producer, Don Fedderson, hears about my gag and says let's change it, it's not funny. But now I haven't got time to tell Newhart, since our dressing rooms are too far apart and he's about to go on.

"I run out and introduce him and he looks at me kind of funny, because I didn't say the line. And just as I'm trotting off following a red carpet that leads to the wooden stairs, someone moves the stairs to another spot—and I can't see because of the bright lights. I'm still following the red carpet and—I land on the cement floor, *ten feet* from the stage. On my noggin!

"People are rushing over and saying, are you all right, and don't sue, we'll fix it, etc. And some of the audience are mumbling. It's scary and very embarrassing. But, naturally, I'm OK."

"What do you mean, *naturally* OK?" Mac asks.

"I guess because I landed soft," I said. "When you've had a few shooters, you land *soft*."

The group seemed impressed.

I've always wondered what Bob Newhart thought when he heard I fell off the stage after introducing him. And remind me to send a note to Bing explaining the art of landing soft.

16

A Song Is Born

ALONG WITH THE IMMORTAL Uniform-of-the-Day, the Story Record, and warm and wonderful Helen Trump, our 15-year-old continuing soap opera, there is a takeoff on the Tin Pan Alley musicians of the good old days called "A Song Is Born," occasionally featured on my morning outrage. It features Foster Brooks, the famous nondrinker who does the world's funniest drunk act. Also, he's a helluva baritone.

I've told you before the story of how Foster used to kill us gigglers at Lakeside with his drunk act and other great impressions and how I invited him to do bits on my program (only for scale) and how he was so grateful. Grateful?! I'm the guy who's grateful. I couldn't afford Foster Brooks in a million rating periods if he didn't regard me as his good friend and golfing buddy. I mean, he gets enough work these days in Las Vegas and on television variety shows without trying to help Old Loudmouth hold up his ratings.

Anyway, Foster still records these tremendously funny vignettes and sketches with me almost weekly. He even flies in from Las Vegas on days off when he's appearing there.

He continues to do it despite what I did to him recently, too. Playing golf at Lakeside, he was kissed by the Whittinghill curse—pulling a stunt that I might do after having a few shooters too many. Trying to play a downhill lie, Foster cracked an anklebone just before opening night in Vegas. As it turned out, he joined the act later in the week on crutches.

Poor Foster. And to think I never had even a tiny bruise after falling out of the golf cart on a hot afternoon, shirtless, and rolling 20 feet into a sandtrap. But that's another story.

Foster does four characters on the program besides his role in "A Song Is Born." He plays Lush, the town drunk; Goofy, the village idiot; Sarah, the inquisitive little girl, and the Old-Timer, the resident lecher.

But "A Song Is Born" is perhaps the best sketch, since it takes some production work and a lot of clever writing and, of course, ad-libbing, which Foster is a master at.

The idea of "A Song Is Born" is the old gag where two guys are having coffee and one of them comes up, almost accidentally, with the lyric to a tune. And it becomes a hit standard. But we give this clichéd scene from a 1940s musical a little satiric twist. In the conversation leading up to the hit tune the songwriters are about to compose, one of them recites lyrics from a known standard. Neither of them picks up on it.

The following is a script from one of our best and most recent collaborations. I play Fred Linley and Foster plays Kurt Brite:

A SONG IS BORN   "Five Foot Two, Eyes of Blue"
NARRATOR: (After a short silence) And now . . . A Song Is Born.
MUSIC: (up and under)
NARRATOR: Yes, here is the true and moving story behind the

creation of another great hit. A song that, only yesterday, all America was singing! The year is 1934. The place: a small mid-town café where two amateur songwriters, Fred Linley and Kurt Brite, are huddled over a cup of coffee.

MUSIC AND SOUND: (Fade music. Establish café noises, followed by a small splash and clink.)

KURT: Fred, you don't look too good. What's the matter?

FRED: Oh, I lost my girl friend.

KURT: It's too bad. What did she look like?

FRED: Golly, Kurt, I'm really sorry. The spoon slipped right out of my hand.

KURT: Yeh, and right into my alphabet soup. Oh, well, it figures. Haven't been able to find my girl for three days.

KURT: (Continuing . . .) Five foot two, Eyes of blue, Has anybody seen my girl? Turned up nose, Turned down hose, Has anybody seen my girl?

FRED: No I'm terribly sorry. I don't know anyone like that.

KURT: Hey, you know something? I've got a letter in my ear!

FRED: Kurt, say that again!

KURT: You dropped a spoon in my alphabet soup and I think I've got a letter in my ear.

FRED: (Picking it up, singing) It makes it very difficult to hear.

KURT: You say you see an L.

FRED: (Singing) You say you see an O.

KURT: You say you see a V and then an E.

FRED: Why, that's LOVE. Heaven's above!

KURT: Imagine having love in your ear!

FRED: Sweet dolly baby!

KURT AND FRED: Imagine having LOVE in your ear!

FRED: Another smasheroo! Waitress . . . over here. Some paper and pencil, please!

KURT: It's us for the Big Time, ol' buddy!

MUSIC: (up)

NARRATOR: You've been listening to A SONG IS BORN, the story behind the immortal Linley-Brite composition: "I Think I've Got a Letter in My Ear!"

MUSIC: (out)

17

Shut Up and Play the Music

THERE ARE VERY FEW pure disc jockeys left in the business these days. I mean, announcers who build their programs around music and limit their comments to music and recording artists. Gone are the Peter Potters, Alex Coopers, Gene Normans, and Al Jarvises.

Today we have the *personality*, generally a euphemism for *comedian*, which means he's an out-of-work comedian who is doing his nightclub act between records. Offhand, the only comedian I can think of who came out of the disc jockey ranks is the incredibly versatile Steve Allen. It should be noted right here that Allen is a musician, too, and that made him a *real* disc jockey in his early days in Phoenix and Hollywood.

In the days before hard rock, these pure disc jockeys were admired and respected for their knowledge of music and their clout—their ability to *make* a hit record. However, let us establish up front that it wasn't their business to make hit records out of bad music. These fellows took professional pride in their knowledge of music and their influence in the music scene.

Peter Potter, who once worked on my station, was so respected as a hit-maker that he enjoyed a long-running television series, "Juke Box Jury," on which guest celebrities would vote on new recordings.

Gene Norman was locally famous for his pop (when it was *pop*) and jazz concerts at various night clubs in Los Angeles—many of them at the Crescendo where you would hear Ella Fitzgerald, Sarah Vaughan, Anita O'Day, June Christy, and other evergreen artists.

Al Jarvis's "Make Believe Ballroom," one of radio's best and oldest record shows, also became a local television hit—one of the first dance party programs. He was the Dick Clark of his day.

Now we have personalities and *formats*—rigid formats—and guys running up and down the halls with rating books and talking out of the sides of their mouths about *demographics* and *tune-outs* and Number Ten with a bullet—a bullet, or big black dot, next to a song on the "hot 100" list means it is on the way up, baby!

I can tell you my philosophy about formats and how I think a disc jockey show should be conducted in one easy lesson. If you have any nephews or nieces or cousins or out-of-work brothers-in-law who are aspiring to become disc jockeys, call them up right now or have these pages Xeroxed. Class is now in session.

My format is the simplest format of all time. Let's capsulize it into a half-hour presentation. You may start off with an instrumental, then a ballad, boy singer, girl singer, etc. The main thing is: something for everyone. I know this sounds cliched, but this is my format.

We're on the air . . . and the record you are hearing now should be different in tempo, attitude, and feeling than the one played before or after it. My feeling is that every record played should create an *experience* for the listener. You are experiencing something. Maybe it's nostalgic, perhaps it's the rhythm, but you are experiencing something. Therefore, the record played afterward should not be the same type. On many rock stations the music is all alike (da-da-da, da-da-da, da-da-da, yeah, yeah, yeah). That is wrong. (*You*, there, pay attention, or Old Whit will slap you across the knuckles with his baton.)

You want another experience? Maybe you're traveling around in a car and you think to yourself, I enjoyed that, now I'm ready for something else. If you follow my format, so utterly simple, you will within that half-hour have something for everybody.

Another point: never *introduce* a record unless you are setting up a new release. For two reasons. (1) The recording artists who made that record—composers and technicians, everyone—had something in mind, like lyrics, verse, bridge, a beginning, middle, and end (most good tunes have these). They've set a tone for this record, a mood. So a good record will have an intro in two or four bars or maybe eight. By listening to it you get in the mood for whatever the artist is going to sing. Why should some loudmouth clown damage that mood by screaming over the record, "Hi, there, dudes and chickies, this is Hammerin' Cameron with all the good sounds . . ." You'd swear the guy announcing over it thought he was more important than the intro. (2) Keep the audience off balance. Remember, there is no right-to-know in radio. The less the listener knows, the better off you are. I go on the radio to sell commercials; I couldn't care less whether a record is selling. So many format stations, particularly rock, say it won't be good unless it sells a lot. I don't believe this at all. If you play something that's beautiful, good, or melodic, that's fine, all you need. But I sell commercials, I *do* want people to listen to the commercials.

If the listener doesn't *buy*, it reflects on the sponsor and he won't buy time—and then, fellow deejays, you may play all the records and *heavy hits* you desire. In order to have your audience hear the commercial, you don't let it know what's coming up. The amateurs say, "In a minute you're going to hear from John Denver, but first this message . . ." I don't care how many people are listening. What if one person out there does not like John Denver? You're giving him the opportunity to tune out, thus completely missing the *commercial*.

Come out of something and go right into the record. The audience is now set up to hear the commercial, or nowadays two or three commercials, before it hears the next record. If a listener doesn't like John Denver, let him tune out, he's heard the two commercials. What do you think would happen if, before a television series broke for a commercial, the station announcer said, "Stay tuned after this message and watch Starsky and Hutch catch the killer"? Someone out there is bound to tune out.

End of crash disc jockey course.

Years ago disc jockeys would have music meetings and vote on current records. They had control of their programs. Why? They *knew* music. Perhaps we would agree to "get on" a certain tune, and on other records some would play it and some wouldn't, depending on their styles. Each disc jockey's program was his *own*. And that's the way it should be *if you have competent people*.

Unfortunately, the *program department* has assumed this task in today's radio. One or two individuals at most every station set themselves up as complete authority on music—judging what should be played and what should *not* be played, with emphasis on the latter. Supposedly, they have knowledge of music, but most of them can't find middle C on a piano. I find it demeaning that someone with inferior credentials wields the power to tell a professional what he can play when the disc jockey himself knows 100 percent more about music.

"Hey, Mr. Gene Autry—play me or trade me."

Huge lines extend around the block as Whit's guests for John Wayne movie (guests had to come handcuffed to partner for admittance).

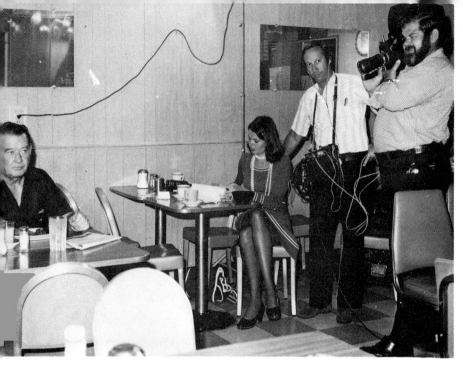

Sandy Hill of Channel 7 doing story on my daily breakfast (must have been a slow news day).

City Councilman Joel Wachs presenting me with a commendation for something or other.

Unveiling of "Whittinghill" for the Hollywood Wax Museum.

Annette Funicello calls on Whit.

Snoopy thinks I'm Woodstock.

Interviewing Forrest Tucker during remote before Whit Golf Tournament.

Foster Brooks (something about the drink?).

Part of the line at autograph party for my first book.

Found an overgrown leprechaun at St. Patrick's Day appearance.

An Anniversary present for the wives.

Program
Director Bob
Forward reviews
my early ratings.

Will the real dummy please stand up?

Here, I strike my best concert pose . . . eat your heart out, Sinatra!

Viking Steward Lud (left) officiates as Whittinghill becomes Chief of the Vikings of Scandia.

Old Whit chats with Bob Newhart and Chairman of the Board Gene Autry at KMPC's annual show of the World Charity Spectacular.

Old Loudmouth and friend at a charity function.

The Brothers Whittinghill (from left, Bud, Dr. John, Bob and Old Whit) before Grudge Match at Lakeside Golf Club of Hollywood.

Arnold Palmer gets a fairway driving tip from Whit. Nice slice, Arnie.

The family in the annual Santa Claus Lane Parade in Hollywood.

The family at the Fourth of July fireworks show. Who says I never take them anywhere?

Cooking and serving food for the multiple sclerosis kids at a Scandia Vikings Benefit.

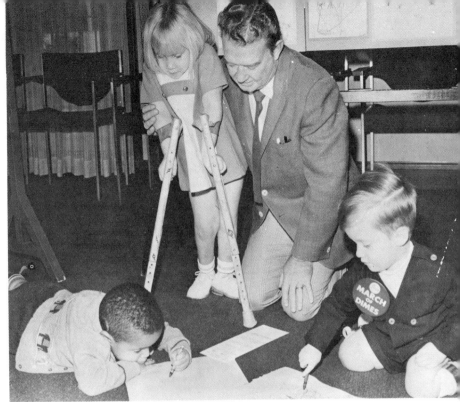

Serving as Southern California Chairman for the March of Dimes.

Whit at a Benefit with Les Brown and Bob Hope.

Old Loudmouth giving some one-liners to emcee Pat Buttram before he does awards program.

Whit appears on Dennis James's TV show with the late Jack Cassidy and Shirley Jones.

When Carol Burnett sees this, she'll say, "How did that guy get in here?"

Up to my hips in grass on an Irish golf course. Lakeside was never like this.

"Ah, yes, it looks like my ball."

Greg Morris and me . . . This mission is impossible. He drinks more than I do!

These music experts who control the disc jockeys usually program by grabbing *Billboard*'s hit list or they phone around town and find out what's selling—regardless of whether it's good or bad music!

If you have a program director who knows what he's doing—who is musically based—it's a plus. And in all fairness, there are a great many young people coming into radio as deejays these days who don't know Tony Bennett from Tony Galento (and they don't know the latter at all). But a sharp P.D. can help a youngster with his music.

Most of the young deejays, and, sadly, too many of today's veterans, believe they're superior to the music. They can't wait for the record to end so they can flog their egos.

The secret is not knowing what to say or when to say it. The secret is knowing when *not* to say it. Let's say a fellow happens to be funny or at least interestingly glib. It's better to have him do two jokes, bits or one-liners, than to blow the whole act in one day. People will remember one or two good jokes longer than one joke lost in an avalanche of strained patter. Here's another tip that relates to what I've just stated. A good disc jockey doesn't have to *work* that hard. What he forgets, as do the alleged program directors, is that 80 percent of the talent is on the record. And I've always believed that 90 percent of all deejays talk too much. They just don't know when to get off!

Perhaps, if you've followed my daily outrage all these years, you'd like to know what this ancient disc jockey likes music-wise.

It's no secret I like brass, being an old trumpet player from high school days in Helena. Trumpets and trombones, good brass. I still play loud and pretty, I think, whenever we have a session at Lakeside, particularly the annual Lakeside clambake where our musical group, which includes actor Buddy Rogers on trombone, gets together.

My early favorites were horn players like Harry James,

Ziggy Ellman, Yank Lawson, and Bix Beiderbecke (although he was before my time). Liking brass so much makes me lament the fact that we don't get good instrumentals on record anymore. Again, it troubles me that a whole generation has grown up listening to absolutely putrid music. Slow down Whittinghill, you've said this all before . . .

Favorite singers? Well, of course, Sinatra leads the list. There is only one Frank and I like everything he's ever done. I think he's a splendid fellow. I won't see him for years and then I'll receive a nice note from him thanking me for playing one of his songs. That's rare these days, believe me.

Of all the fine things that Sinatra has done my very favorite is "Baby Won't You Please Come Home." His phrasing on that record is impeccable, superb. It wasn't a big hit, but it was a perfect recording.

On the distaff side, other vocalists I like are Ella Fitzgerald, Jo Stafford, Eydie Gorme, and Vikki Carr. Now, if you're under 30 (what are you doing reading this?), you'll call me an old poop. I am not old.

Songs that have influenced me? Too many. I have too many favorites. Do my wife and I have a love song, you ask? Oh, yes. Let me tell you about it.

In our college days in Montana, Willy and I used to dance cheek to cheek to "Good Night Sweetheart." We first heard it dancing together on a date in East Helena on a moonlit night. We were dancing close when the band played it, and I got goose bumps and the warmies. I looked into her eyes, she looked into mine, and I knew, *we knew*, this was *our song*.

It was always *our song*.

It wasn't till many, many years later that Willy told me it was also *their song*—that of Willy and the other guy she went with in college before she met me. I was irate. But we kept "Good Night Sweetheart" anyway.

18

Rooney . . . as in Looney

MICKEY ROONEY is one of the nicest and craziest guys I've ever met, and I love to play golf with him, even though he ruins my game for weeks by giving me his secret pointers.

Mickey likes to call me up on the air during records. I have a private line directly into Studio B where I do my program. Other members of my *first team* report in almost daily. I usually get a call from Beban right after he shaves, about 6:07 A.M. Then Caruso will call in with news of his day's itinerary—a murder case, a big suit, whatever. Then I hear from various others, maybe even Willy or Nora with a shopping list. I feel like I'm the den mother or social chairman for all my buddies.

I always hear from Rooney when he wants to play golf. "Widdlediddle, how about a golf game . . . Whiffinpoofer, I'm going to show you something that'll take four strokes off your game . . ."

When Rooney isn't calling to set up a game, he'll call with the latest joke.

The other day, between 7:00 and 8:00 A.M., Rooney calls from *Dallas, Texas*.

"Whittledingle, I've got a story for you!"

"Fine, Mick, but can't it wait until tomorrow. We're playing golf, remember?"

"No, Whippleflipple, it can't wait. This is a classic and I want you to be the first guy in L. A. to tell it—on the air."

"Make it fast, I've got a commercial coming up in two minutes."

Rooney's story:

"Two tourists are looking over the edge of the Grand Canyon, and one of them spots something way down on the canyon floor.

"'What's that down there?' one asks.

"'Looks like a dead burro,' the other guy says.

"So, they go down a trail to the canyon floor and sure enough, it's a dead burro.

"'You take its hind legs and I'll lift its head and we'll bury it,' one says.

"As they're lifting the burro up they discover a Mexican lying there moaning and groaning.

"'Gosh, we better get this poor guy to a hospital fast,' they say.

"Then they roll the Mexican over and there's something written on his T-shirt.

"It says: 'EVEL GONZALES.'"

The next day Mickey is telling the joke to everyone we meet at Lakeside before I've had my chance.

19

The Great Montague

IF I'VE GOT A CHAPTER titled "Rooney as in Looney," I must devote a line or two to the Great Montague.

Montague was a legendary guy who hung around Lakeside for about two decades. He was one of the strongest men I ever knew. Just playing around in the men's grille one day, he picked Oliver (Babe) Hardy up with *one arm* and sat him down on the bar! It scared Babe to death.

Montague could hit a golf ball into orbit. He had arms like Mighty Joe Young. No one knew what he did for a living, but he probably hustled guys at other clubs because he was a phenomenal golfer and a real flakey individual. Colorful, I suppose. One day he'd have pockets full of money and the next day he'd be mooching drinks and borrowing money. Montague could drink, too. I don't mean imbibe. I mean *drink*.

He was always pulling stunts on the golf course and getting his name in the sports pages. I wasn't on hand for his most famous stunt, but if you're a golfer you'll appreciate it. Montague once played an entire round of golf with a shovel and a rake. So what's so funny about that? Well, playing with a shovel and a rake is odd. But shooting in the *80s* is even more unbelievable.

I'm not going to say anything more about him because the Great Montague is dead. I wish he wasn't. He owes me a lot of money.

20

My Favorite Story Records

YEARS AND YEARS AGO when you and I were young, there was an audience that liked to be told humorous stories. And the morning elf on KMPC devised cute little stories that would have punch lines from songs on record.

In those early years I was writing five story records a day. It was becoming too much, so I turned the bit over to my listeners. And it became The Story Record. We've had a story record every day since then and give out nice prizes for the winning, or best, story record of the week.

Thousands of story records have spun off the turntable through the years and I've tried to remember some of the good ones to put down for posterity here (in case they ever erect a disc jockey's hall of fame).

The punch lines to these stories don't precisely match the lyric, but the words can be imagined to sound the same.

For example: A guy is visiting the county coroner. While they're talking, the one guy discovers that the Miss Los

Angeles Beauty Contest is being held in the next room, but the door is locked. However, the transom is open. Thinking fast, he asks the coroner to bend over so he can see the girls. "What are you doing?" the coroner's secretary says. Punch line from record: "Standing on the Cor-ner, watching all the girls go by. . ."

A little kangaroo is using his mother's pouch as an office for cashing checks. Pretty soon he calls over his friend, a little porcupine, to cash the checks while the little kangaroo goes to the bathroom. But mama kangaroo objects. "Forget it," she says. The little kangaroo says, "Why?" Punch line: "Only you can make this change in me. . ."

A cow is about to give birth to twin calves. But only one slips out. The other is born later on. Years later the twins meet and compare notes. Discovering he has a twin, the second-born says: "Why did you go away and leave me in Big Maamoo?"

Perhaps the all-time favorite story record of mine and most listeners is about Adam and Eve. It goes this way: Adam and Eve are in the Garden of Eden one day and Adam has to relieve himself. So he scampers into a wooded area to do so. Eve, always curious, sneaks over and peeks through the bushes. While watching Adam do his number, she thinks to herself, "HE'S GOT THE WHOLE WORLD IN HIS HANDS."

You get the idea . . .

21

My Favorite Uniforms-of-the-Day (...and their social significance)

I DON'T KNOW HOW IT STARTED. In fact, I don't know how half the things I do start on my show. I get a sudden inspiration and let fly. It seems to build insanely.

So the uniform-of-the-day came in somewhere between the soap opera ("Helen Trump") and "Did you Whittinghill this morning?" — which was a moderately successful campaign, don't you think?

We were having a heat wave in Los Angeles and it was 80 degrees by eight in the morning. And I said something like, "Well, girls, it's going to be a scorcher, so dress accordingly. Let's see. How about a sunbonnet, a bikini, and sandals?"

Innocent enough, right?

I did this for a couple more days and then the listeners started writing in and I had suggestions from my friends. Everyone was coming up with cute uniforms to match the weather. "A halter, short shorts, and mucklucks." "A white sheet with holes in the knees." "Suspenders and army boots."

"Straw hat and wooden shoes." "Raincoat and snowshoes." You know, silly stuff.

By now I was calling it the uniform-of-the-day and of course I got carried away and my evil little mind took over.

I remember one of the first crazy uniforms I devised, which opened the floodgates for my equally evil-minded colleagues and friends:

"OK, here's the uniform-of-the-day for wives and sweethearts of college professors. You wear a necklace of McGuffy's Readers, two dangling participles, and a split infinitive!" I could almost hear the program director racing down the hall.

People began whispering, "Did you *hear* Whittinghill's uniform-of-the-day this morning?" It was being passed around like a stick of dynamite.

Another classic arrived after I broke the ice. Art Aragon, Los Angeles's Golden Boy of boxing, dispatched this one: "Wives, sweethearts, and friends of professional fighters will wear a necklace of eye swabs, two speed bags, and a split decision." I changed the latter to read "ring apron."

Paul Caruso, who once got Aragon out of jail in the great fix scandal that never came off, or wasn't, followed with this: "Wives and sweethearts of all attorneys will wear a necklace of bench warrants, two depositions and an open-and-shut case." I've never fully understood that one.

Bill Hipple, our Irish tour guide, submitted one: "Wives and sweethearts of airline pilots will wear a stewardess's cap, two barf bags, and a c--------!" It was too X-rated to even put down on paper. I changed it, too.

A regular listener had another classic: "Wives and sweethearts of bowlers will wear a necklace of spares, two turkeys, and a seven-ten split." Everybody seemed so preoccupied with coming up with a borderline tag. It was sort of electronic beaver shooting.

One of my golfing buddies dispatched the obvious: "Wives

and sweethearts of golfers will wear a necklace of tees, two mashies, and a divot." Many fans sent in the same uniform only with the last part being "a hole-in-one." But I was getting bad enough without that kind of help.

But you get the idea.

When you read this, jot down your uniform-of-the-day and send it along. This will probably go on forever.

But don't you get the picture of some $100,000-a-year executive sitting up in his office late at night giggling and scratching and writing down various uniforms-of-the-day that verge on the indecent while his stockholders toss and turn in their sleep?

Only in Hollywood.

22

The Great Fillmore Expedition
(... taking the act out of town)

THE WORST TWO GOLFERS I've ever played with are attorney Paul Caruso and Don Page, the writer. If it went to a committee, Page would probably get the vote as the worst of the two.

Caruso, a 30 handicap, is usually lying 4 with a chip shot remaining to get on the green. Page is usually lying 4, also. But that's off the *tee*. I've never seen anything like it. Page is six-foot-five, weighs around 240 pounds, has a pretty swing but can't hit the ball off the tee. When he does, it's the biggest slice you ever saw. No one can figure it out. Even the pros won't touch him, anymore. "Please don't tell anyone you took lessons from me," they plead.

When Page plays at Lakeside, he spends more time in the trees than Tarzan. When they see him approaching the green, the caddies whistle "Mr. Sandman." He's been places at Lakeside that no golfer has ever been. And on top of all this, Page can't keep score. He can be gone for half an hour off the tee, then emerge from the trees calling, "I'm lying five!" And Caruso says, "Well, you're half right." Page has made Jim Murray's all-time golfing greats list as The Scorer (as in beware of).

Caruso, who had 44 amateur fights and has had his Sicilian nose broken five times, is also pugnacious on the course. He doesn't play often but plays hard and concentrates, always forging ahead. Unlike Page, Caruso is usually inbounds. But Caruso does whiff more often than the big writer.

When we play (with Murray, always), I tell them they have to pick up after four strokes if they aren't on the green because it's embarrassing and we hold up other foursomes, who sometimes complain. I even announce it on my morning program. "All you guys planning to play golf today at Lakeside had better tee off before noon, because the Fearsome Foursome is playing today—Caruso, Murray, Whittinghill, and Page."

Murray is a fair golfer, pretty good on his best days, but he loses his all-important concentration when he hooks up with Caruso and Page. They talk a lot and needle each other, and Murray can't concentrate. It becomes part-irritation, part-laughing, distraction.

"Fun is fun," Murray will grumble, "but dammit Dynamite, (Page's nickname), there's no way you had a seven back there. It was at least a nine!" This is funny because Murray and Page are partners.

The last time we toured Lakeside, Caruso came in with 125 and Page had (a fanfare, please . . .) 147! Can you imagine how long it took to play that round? The entire Masters doesn't last as long. Standard equipment for the Fearsome Foursome includes a flask, flashlights, and a Sherpa guide. I generally tip well, but when I bring along Caruso and Page, the caddies actually hide. Their wives and kids have been known to beg them not to go to work when I announce the Fearsome Foursome is having a party at Lakeside.

In view of this, and out of shame, Page volunteered to become activity chairman of the group and suggested we take the act out of town, get away from Lakeside for a change. Perhaps less pressure would improve our game, he thought. I reminded him that there was nothing much wrong with *our* game when he and Caruso weren't with us. But Page sandbagged us into a golfing safari, a fairway expedition 50 miles from Lakeside, in Fillmore, California. Fillmore is one huge orange grove nestled at the foot of a beautiful range of mountains. I'd never been there, neither had Page, but he had heard wonderful things about Fillmore's course—Elkins Ranch.

"You hit a ball, eat an orange," Page said. He said many of his friends play at Elkins Ranch and love it.

Well, we agreed to it. We were to meet at Lakeside, have a few shooters, and Caruso would chauffeur us to Fillmore in his royal purple Rolls-Royce. Caruso isn't your average divorce lawyer. Zsa Zsa Gabor, Pamela Mason, and other movie stars have had their knots untied by the Beverly Hills barrister. And many famous athletes have utilized his legal genius. Other attorneys drive Cadillacs. Caruso drives—or is driven in—a Rolls-Royce. His chauffeur and man Friday is Roger Leighton, former fight manager who once handled the lightweight champion of the world, Lauro Salas.

Also joining the group this day was my old boss, Bob Forward, now an actor of note. You may remember him as the chief hospital administrator in the television series, "Marcus Welby, M.D." Forward, having heard about our legendary foursome, had asked to come along as an impartial observer. How depressing, Caruso and Page have made us a *novelty act.*

It was gray and misty as the purple Rolls sped through the hinterlands toward Fillmore. It seemed like it took all day, but we arrived at Elkins Ranch at 11:30 A.M., just five minutes late for our starting time. Gazing about us, we observed that the course was carved out on the sides of two mountains and we were completely surrounded by orange trees. Well, this would be an adventure. With Caruso and Page playing *this* course, we might have to send telegrams to our wives. Or, drop leaflets. Or wear instructions to the Red Cross on the backs of our jackets.

In the starter's office, we were greeted by a grouchy individual who warned us not to be late again and mumbled something about doing us a favor by letting us tee off five minutes late.

Before teeing off on No. 1, we advanced on the clubhouse (or cafeteria) for liquid reinforcements. To our horror, we discovered that the place was dry. They served only beer.

"I'm a million miles from home out in the middle of nowhere and Page picks a dry hole!" Murray sputters.

Immediately, Caruso summoned Leighton and Roger was sent into town on a mission of mercy. Bring back the booze!

On the first tee, Page grunts and slices one out of bounds into the thickly wooded hillside. He takes a Mulligan. Now he hits another ball that slices right and angles *over* the hillside. You had to see it to believe it.

We're taking a long time getting started and a voice booms over the public address system: "Will the Page foursome on the first tee get moving, please. You're holding up two foursomes." The words echoed off the mountains and it was embarrassing.

Both Caruso and Page are out-of-bounds on the partly uphill fourth fairway (sounds just like "Wide World of Sports," doesn't it?). Already, we've been out here an hour and there are foursomes behind us with guys standing around with their arms folded.

At last, Leighton arrives with the sauce, plus mixes, and a block of ice.

"A *block* of ice?" Caruso chirps.

"Yeah, Paul," Leighton says, "they don't have ice cubes to go in Fillmore. There are no bars open, either."

"Primitive," Forward, the observer, says.

We all wonder how we make ice cubes out of a block of ice?

"Hand me your nine-iron," Forward says. He takes a hefty woodchopper's swing. . .

CRAAAAAACCCKKKK!

Sheepishly, Forward hands me my bent nine-iron.

"I had a helluva time getting this stuff in here," Leighton says. "The manager came running out of his office and started jumping up and down yelling 'No liquor allowed on the course!' And I told him, this is *lunch*. That's all. Lunch. All the while the bottles are clanging and gurgling as I'm hauling them over here."

"Not much of a sport, is he," says Caruso.

"Not only that," Leighton continues, "but he says he's going to throw us off the course because we sneaked in a fifth player. I told him Forward was just watching. And he says they don't allow watchers, either. I ignored him."

Murray finally slam-dunked the block of ice on the cart path and produced several cup-sized chunks of ice and we made a few shooters and continued our jolly game.

Page unleashed a mighty drive off the tee on No. 7, slicing it slightly, but the ball came to rest just 30 feet from the pin. Page had the opportunity for the first eagle of his life! This was unbelievable, since he's still waiting for the first *par* of his life. Coolly, he proceeds to five-putt the green for a double-bogey.

Murray is laughing so hard, he three-putts for a bogey.

As we approach No. 9, halfway around the mountain, I note we've been on the course for three hours. Caruso holes out with a 52, Murray and I are tied with 42s, and Page is in with 72!

"If we stop now," Murray says, "We'll tell everyone Page had a 72, but we won't reveal it was for *nine* holes."

"Yeah, I want to get back before my family files a missing person report," Caruso adds.

Halfway home, we stop at a saloon off Interstate 5; it looks like a spot where the Rotarians meet every Thursday for lunch. The drinks were weaker than the St. Louis Browns. After one round we're preparing for the stretch run back to Lakeside and Page says, "Wait till you see the course I've picked out for us next time."

Right then, he was stripped of his title of activity chairman. We're going to stay at Lakeside. But Page can't play in the Fearsome Foursome until he breaks 110.

Mercifully, the rest of us will be long gone by then.

23

My Friend, Bucky . . .
(Rin-Tin-Tin, he ain't)

YOU MIGHT KNOW that someone as peculiar as I am would have some strange pets. My home has been the dwelling for dogs, cats, fish, squirrels, butterflies, and even a boa constrictor named Pinky. All of them were eccentric. But the most eccentric of all was Bucky, our German Shepherd, who now lives with daughter Nora in Medford, Oregon.

Actually, Bucky's real name is Dick Butkus, after the maniacal linebacker of the Chicago Bears, who does a lot of acting in TV commercials these days. Why did we name him Dick Butkus? Of course.

Anyway, after we hung the name on him it occurred to me that we couldn't call him that in public. I mean, my wife couldn't go out on the porch at night and yell, "Come here, *Dick*!" Or "*Dick*, don't you dare do *that* on the rosebushes out there!" The neighbors would think, what on earth is wrong with this guy Dick? So we called him Bucky.

Bucky was big, lovable, and slobbered all over you when

you gave him attention. And, I guess, he was sort of simple.

He never learned to romp around the neighborhood with the other dogs, and he never learned to jump the white picket fence around our big corner lot. It is only three feet high, but Bucky couldn't get over it. Bucky was very popular with the other dogs and they would jump over our fence and play with him. They'd run and laugh and go to the bathroom with him in the yard. Then they would leap back over the fence, woof at him to go with them, and run home. Bucky would put his front paws on the fence and stare after them. He couldn't jump that little fence, or maybe he figured he had a good thing going at home with the three squares a day and a lot of petting.

Another thing was lacking in Bucky's repertoire—he didn't know how to lift his leg to go to the bathroom, like all normal male dogs. He'd spread out like a female and I was always embarrassed for him. I wondered what all of his friends thought? So, I kept trying to teach him by hitting his right hind leg and telling him, "Bucky, go to the bathroom." But with all my coaching, he'd trot over to his favorite tree, look at it, and spread his legs out. He never came close to the tree!

One night Bucky and I are watching the six o'clock news and I'm having a few shooters, naturally, and I decide I've had it with his girlish way of going to the bathroom.

"Willy," I call out, "I'm going to show Bucky how to go to the bathroom; I'll be back in a few minutes."

"Sure, Whit," she says.

So Bucky and I toddle off to the front yard toward Bucky's favorite walnut tree that he never hits.

"Now, Bucky, you just watch me. I'm going to show you *how* to go to the bathroom like a male dog should. Your friends are going to think you're gay if you don't stop that stupid spreading out routine.

"Watch me, Bucky. Come over here, now." I whacked him on his right hind leg. Then I whacked my right leg. I was down on all fours. "See, Bucky. Go-to-the-bathroom." I show him.

I whack him. I whack me. I lift my leg. He looks at me, panting happily. I show him. I whack him. I whack me. I lift my leg. "Bucky, go-to-the-bathroom."

You know that slow, burning feeling that creeps up your back and rings your ears when you feel that someone is watching you? It sort of crept up on me as I was raising my leg again. I looked up, gritting my teeth.

There was a nice elderly couple standing there watching me. I looked at them. They seemed very interested, kind of craning their necks. I looked at Bucky. He was watching me, with his head kind of tilted to one side.

I got up and ran into the house.

"What's the matter, Whit?" Willy asked.

"Oh, nothing," I said.

I peeked out the curtains. The couple was still standing there. Bucky was still standing there. The three of them were staring at the window.

When I put Bucky on the plane for Oregon to go and live with newly married Nora and her husband, Bill Murphy, I was as sorry to see him leave as I was Nora. I knew I'd see Nora again, but it was doubtful that I'd see Bucky again. But Bucky didn't let me down. Soon after he settled in Medford, he made headlines!

The following is a wire service report:

(MEDFORD)—TELEVISION NEWSMAN BILL MURPHY TOOK THE WORD OF FRIENDS THAT PEOPLE AROUND MEDFORD USUALLY CHOOSE THE FUN OF HARVESTING THEIR OWN CHRISTMAS TREE OVER THE EXPENSE OF BUYING THEM.

HE GOT A U.S. FOREST SERVICE PERMIT FOR $1, THEN:

—HE DROVE 100 MILES ROUND-TRIP TO THE PERMIT AREA AND BACK.

—HE LOST IN THE SNOW THE HANDSAW HE BORROWED FROM HIS LANDLORD AND HAD TO REPLACE IT.

—HE HELPED HIS WIFE THROUGH THREE TRIPS TO A DERMATOLOGIST AND THREE DAYS OFF WORK BECAUSE SHE GOT POISON OAK ON THE EXPEDITION.

—HE DISCOVERED AFTER WORK ONE DAY THAT HIS 95-POUND GERMAN SHEPHERD HAD EATEN MUCH OF THE TREE, BY THEN VALUED AT $175.

MURPHY SAID, "THE DOG HAS TAKEN UP PERMANENT RESIDENCE IN THE GARAGE, AND WE'LL JOYFULLY CELEBRATE CHRISTMAS BY PUTTING OUR PACKAGES AROUND OUR VERY EXPENSIVE CHRISTMAS STUMP."

And that's my friend, Bucky.

24

A Very Alarming Situation

WHEN WE MOVED INTO our big white house in a pleasant, middle-upper-class section of North Hollywood, it wasn't long before a fellow came along to offer us a security system against burglars and prowlers. I thought it was a splendid idea, especially since the installer wasn't going to charge the installee anything.

The man had never installed a burglar-alarm system in homes before, so ours was to be the prototype to lure prospective customers for him. Besides, it seemed like an intelligent thing to do since we had small children running around the house. And Willy and I had collected some valuable household furnishings over the years, and there were several television sets, along with a well-stocked wine cellar.

The original system—it's more sophisticated now—had photoelectric beams all over the place that would set off an alarm you could hear for blocks.

Well, you guessed it, we were always setting it off by mistake. I'd come home late, forgetting that it was on, and the stupid bell would go on and so would the lights all over the neighborhood. Then the cops would show up and, of course, it was all very embarrassing. Even the cat tripped it by walking by the electric beam with its tail in the air. Cops were coming by with guns drawn at all hours of the day and night. It looked like a location scene for "Starsky and Hutch." Or at that time, "Dragnet."

Finally, we had to redo the whole thing. And guys came out and wrecked walls, ripped things up, and added new paint—at no cost. I was very pleased. The new system is triggered either by someone entering through a window or a door, or by pushing one of many red "panic-buttons" situated at strategic spots throughout the house; den, living room, bathrooms, and bedrooms. It is hooked up to a silent-ringer system relayed to the North Hollywood Police Station. You or the burglar don't know it has been tripped until the cops show up. Getting the picture?

I think I must have set it off about three times before I remembered to shut it off as I entered the house. Then, of course, you reset it upon retiring for the night.

Many times little Willy or Nora would hear me come in, and when I was safely tucked in bed, one of them would yell, "Dad, quick! Turn off the burglar alarm!" I'd have only about 10 seconds to rush and turn it off before the cops arrived. Then reset it with a trembling hand.

Of course, several times the girls' playmates have pushed the little red buttons. "Gee, what's this, Nora and Willy?" Then, a few minutes later, "Nora and Willy, what are all those policemen doing in your front yard with those guns?"

One night we all were sitting in my little den playing cards and I told the family a joke I'd heard at Lakeside, and daughter Willy laughed and leaned back, not knowing she had pressed the panic button. A few minutes later there was this soft knock at the front door. "Oh, golly," Willy said, "I think

I know what *that* is." She opened the door and a cop stood there with a shotgun. "Someone press the button again by accident, honey, or is this the real thing?" he said, with a wink.

I suppose the funniest alarm bit happened not long ago when Wilamet and I were preparing to go out to some big function and I had called for the KMPC limousine and a chauffeur. I know it sounds snobbish, but really it's the only way to go and it's available to me. (When I was driving a beat-up old car in Helena during high school days I never dreamed of a limousine and chauffeur.)

Just before we departed, one of the girls' girl friends had unknowingly leaned against a panic button. It had been a long time since one of those mistakes, so the police couldn't know it wasn't the real thing.

Here's the tableau:

We step out of the front door and Wilamet says, "Whit, what is that policeman doing out there crouched down, running with his gun in his hand?"

And we look around and cops are starting to swarm all over the place and the police helicopter appears overhead with a searchlight trained on the front yard. And here's my limousine driver. The cops have got him spread-eagled over the hood of the car and they're frisking him. Now lights are going on all over the neighborhood and little knots of people are forming on their porches watching all of this bizarre activity.

Willy and I are sort of standing there on the porch hugging each other, when a familiar sergeant comes up the walk with a shotgun. He slowly sizes up the situation, lowers the shotgun, and takes off his hat.

"Oh, hi, Mr. Whittinghill." (Pause) "Mr. Whittinghill . . ."

25

Little Willy, Master Detective

DAUGHTER WILLY HAS ALWAYS been a fast learner. Show her something just once and she becomes an expert. You may recall I taught her how to shake dice in her early, innocent years and before her mother and I could stop her, Willy was running a floating crap game in neighborhood garages. She was happily and without malice taking her sunny-faced playmates for their hard-earned allowances.

We received a lot of phone calls from upset parents, but they understood and Willy made the proper refunds. They understood because they knew Willy's father, Old Bumblepan.

We always tried to provide Willy with something that would occupy her computer-like mind whenever gift-giving was involved.

One Christmas, when she was ten, Mommy and Daddy gave little Willy a fingerprint kit. Naturally, she was thrilled with it and in a short period of time Willy had the fingerprints of practically every child on the block. She had a regular digital rogue's gallery.

After the tiring holidays, we packed up for a short vacation in Palm Springs. Upon our return it was discovered that someone had broken in through one of the upstairs windows and stolen a small amount of money. It was nothing alarming, but since it involved a break-in, we called the police.

"You know how these things are, Mr. Whittinghill," said the sergeant. "It's pretty hard to tell who did it. I mean, there isn't really anything to go on."

"Oh, what about fingerprints?" I asked, squinting skeptically. I had done "Dragnet," you know.

"Well, Mr. Whittinghill, prints dissolve after a couple of days, so there's little chance there, and, well, you're only talking about a few dollars."

I should have realized that the crime was too insignificant to bring in a team of detectives to search for clues, what with the escalating burglary rate and murder, rape, and drugs rampant in our society. I mean, all the Sgt. Fridays of the world have more important things to do like saving lives.

I apologized for taking up the LAPD's valuable time and took out the garbage.

But immediately, daughter Willy got busy. She went over the scene thoroughly with her fingerprint kit, dusting windows, ledges, tables, chairs, bureaus, etc. I smiled and thought to myself, what a busy little bee she is. Give her a toy and she's so happy. I went over to Lakeside to play golf.

"Willy found the burglar, Whit," Wilamet announced as I dropped into my old easychair to watch the evening news.

"Willy-found-the-burglar?" I repeated, amazed. "Who is he, where was it, he, them?" I had visions of the cops sweeping down on some guy and handcuffing him after being identified by my daughter.

"Willy found the prints upstairs and nailed the burglar," Wilamet said, like a desk sergeant.

"You mean she found some prints with that toy fingerprint kit?"

"Yep. And they matched little Marsha's prints."

"Marsha? You mean her little friend down the street?"

"Yep. Remember, she already had a set of prints from all the little kids around here."

"Well, how did she do it? How did she make the, uh . . ."

"The *bust*? Just went over there and showed the prints to Marsha and told her to come clean, and Marsha confessed. Willy forgave her and Marsha gave back the money. Her parents were very upset about the break-in. But everything's OK."

"I'll be darned," I said. "Where is Willy now?"

"Upstairs calling the North Hollywood police. She's going to tell them that she caught the burglar."

Dum-Dee-Dum-Dum!

26

The Little Chalet

I'VE NEVER TAKEN down the dollhouse that Alfonso Badera built for my daughters.

Alfonso is my gardener. He's also a fine bricklayer. He can even build houses.

"I want a dollhouse for my little girls," I told him. "I'll leave the design up to you, Alfonso. But I want it in the side yard there on Christmas morning when Willy and Nora wake up."

I thought little more about it as the holiday season approached since I had every confidence in Alfonso. He has a wonderful touch for everything. The grounds around our house have always looked the freshest in the spring, the brightest in the summertime, and the neatest and cleanest in winter. Everything was safe with Alfonso in charge.

Soon it was Christmas Eve, 1965, and after the children were asleep, Wilamet and I scurried around the house getting everything ready—filling stockings with candy and little gifts and carefully laying out all the big presents under the tree. Then, after a hot toddy, Willy and I retired.

It must have been 2:00 A.M. when I heard it—a peculiar scraping and whooshing sound. I sprang from my bed and ran to the window (wait, that's someone else's line). But what did my eyes see? It was incredible!

Coming along the middle of the street was this structure, this, uh, house! It was being pulled along the street on logs! Under the street lights I could barely make out Alfonso and 16 of his Mexican friends—no one saying a word, moving slowly in the moonlight. It looked like a procession going to Lourdes.

The next morning there it was. The dollhouse. Its red paint and white trimming shining in the sunlight on a gorgeous Christmas morning. It looked like a Swiss chalet. It was almost as big as a guest house!

Well, little Willy and Nora shrieked with delight, running in and out of it and running back and forth to the main house hauling out dolls and toys. By the afternoon they were entertaining their friends at "tea."

All day long I heard from our neighbors who said they had "seen it" coming along the street in the dead of night. It was like they had witnessed a religious ceremony.

The kids loved it, I loved it, and Alfonso was very proud.

But I began to have some problems getting clearance to keep the *chalet* on the property. The woman next door protested that it obstructed her view, or something. Anyway, I went down to City Hall several times with different ideas about how to save it for my daughters.

It seems we couldn't work anything out, but the fellow at City Hall was very pleasant about it, especially since he was a regular listener and a golf nut, too. A golf nut? The wheels in Old Loudmouth's head began to spin. A golf nut.

That very afternoon the man from City Hall and your morning host were on the course at Lakeside and he's having a wonderful time.

Now we're in the bar and we're having a few shooters and he's having an even more wonderful time and becoming quite concerned about the possibility of me losing the dollhouse. And he's becoming more receptive to my ideas.

So I invited him over to the house to see it.

"Gee, it's a beautiful dollhouse," he said, sipping his drink. "Hey, maybe we could put wheels on it. Ya know, move it around if the lady next door complains."

I liked the way he said *we.*

"Or maybe you could put a tree behind it (hic!)"

Willy and Nora began to play in the late afternoon sun, and the sun's rays washed the dollhouse and their happy faces. (How do you like it so far?)

After thinking of three or four more options, the nice man from City Hall said, "We will let you keep it there for one year." He was firm but satisfied with the decision. He smiled and finished his drink.

That was 12 years ago and the little chalet still stands. I'll never take it down, either. Besides, the woman next door moved away and the new residents like it.

Willy and Nora will have children. And they will play in my little chalet.

27

Nora to the Rescue
(. . . if she hadn't come
so late!)

NORA, OUR PIXIE, LIVE-WIRE, and first-married, was always a humorous kid with lots of energy, getting into things, flitting around. She was not a fireball in school, especially in math, so you must understand how shocked and very pleased I was when she ends up practically running a whole lumber company in Oregon! I mean, she deals in board weight and cubic feet, or is it cubic weight and board feet? And does the ordering and bookkeeping and all that stuff. And learned it in one year!

But I'm getting way ahead of this chapter, which is another fond memory of an adventure with my family, and where Nora pulls it off in her own very special spontaneous fashion.

When Willy was eight and Nora six, we took them to Sea World in San Diego. This sounds simple enough. But it wasn't. It never is during our family excursions.

Unlike my troops in the army, my family doesn't follow directions or orders. My family does just the opposite. It's an all-fall-down thing. We're always struggling through crowds and getting lost.

Well, on this particular day we've been touring Sea World since early morning and by now it's 1:00 P.M. and it's getting hot and we're tired and hungry. So we find a cafe'and shove our way through the huge crowd. It looks like it's going to be tough.

"Whit," Wilamet says, "you find a table and I'll take the children to the bathroom."

Good idea, I thought.

Now I'm shouldering my way through the crowd and I spot one, a table! Just as I get to it a guy zooms in and grabs it, sneering at me. So I sneer back and look for another one. Then a fat lady with about 11 children crunches me in flight toward a table. Finally, after knocking over a few people, I discover a table way in back, and I quickly pull the chairs in and sort of surround it. I sigh. Looking around, I don't see my little brood. Where are they?

It's a little embarrassing. I'm almost draped over this table and people are looking at me because it's a self-service café and I'm taking up all this space and not eating.

At last, I see the family coming out of the women's john. I stand up waving. They don't see me. Now I'm hollering and waving. "Willy, over here! Over here, Willy, kids! Here I am! Here, here!"

I can't get their attention, but by now I've got the attention of everybody else in the joint. And they're looking to see who I'm hollering at.

"Hey, Willy!"

The room is silent except for me hollering.

The family finally sees me.

But Mama is waving and gesturing and indicating that we have to go home.

I'm yelling, "No, no! I've got the table. Come over here for lunch!"

The people are looking back and forth like they're watching a tennis match.

Then little Nora, exasperated, cups her hands around her mouth and shouts: "We can't have lunch! We gotta go home! Mama just got her *period*!"

The whole place became a shambles. People were pounding the tables, wilting with laughter.

Now Wilamet is trying to get out the glass door. She can't find the handle and she's *clawing* at the glass. Before I could get there they had disappeared. But I could see marks on the glass door where poor Willy was trying to claw her way to freedom.

Sea World was still laughing as I ran for the car.

28

Thirty Seconds
Over Los Angeles
(... and nobody got hurt)

IN THE OLD DAYS it was common for us disc jockey types to appear on television variety shows or in movies. We lent "authenticity" to the musical theme. One of my first post-Pied Piper invitations to become a thespian came in the early fifties, when the Kid from Montana was selected to represent the West Coast in a film featuring my colleagues from all sections of the country.

I don't remember the name of the picture and I don't know if it ever was released, but the money seemed fair at the time and I had a free, first-class airplane ticket to New York, didn't I?

I recall hearing the news of my selection from Tess Russell, my long time secretary and music librarian, who orchestrates the whole Whittinghill program. After the details were arranged, I told Tess to book me on a Pan Am flight with one of those fancy sleeping berths, which they had in those days. Old Loudmouth was going first cabin to the Great White Way, which actually turned out to be an old, yellowing, dank studio somewhere in southern New York.

At the airport, after checking in my luggage, I repaired to the tower saloon for a few shooters (I wasn't going to get on the plane *alone*), and, having had them, marched happily up the ramp to prepare for the trip.

Feeling good, I climbed up the little ladder to my upper berth as the pretty stewardess smiles and wishes me a pleasant night's sleep. With a nice sleep the 3,000 miles will go by fast.

The berth was narrow and rather cramped as I wrestled and squirmed to untie my shoes. I was in a very odd position, sort of wedged in, struggling, when I finally got my knee in my face and was able to reach one shoe. I could hear the passengers filing on board. My shoe fell somewhere. Then I managed to get the other knee up, gasping. It must have looked like a scene from a Marx Brothers movie. We took off . . .

Suddenly, my body unsprings and I fall out of the berth, right on top of this fellow, crunching his hat. His briefcase popped open and papers were flying through the air and settling on the passengers.

I struggled to my feet, apologizing while fixing his crunched hat. OK, folks, knowing *me*, who would you say I fell onto right after taking off? Orville Wright? Charles A. Lindbergh? General Billy Mitchell? No, but close.

The Old Bumbler from Hollywood fell out of an airplane berth onto General Jimmy Doolittle—a three-star general! The general who led the famous World War II air strike on Japan! The hero of the movie, *Thirty Seconds Over Tokyo*!

He never got an earache from that historical bombing raid, but he gets his hat crunched and knocked down by a disc jockey.

Years later, Willy and I are on a flight to Denver and, what a small sky we fly in, there's General Doolittle sitting right across from us. I introduced myself and, by golly, he remembered me falling on him.

"I didn't think he'd remember." I said to Willy.

"Well, after so many missions during the war," she said, "the Tokyo raid and . . . oh, never mind, Whit."

29

The Magic Mouth

GROWN MEN PLAY SILLY GAMES and I'm one of the best at it. When it comes to pulling off a gag, I'll do almost anything. I'm a disc jockey. It's not a serious business. You want serious, hire Mike Wallace.

One of the silliest games I ever played (and still do to this day) was initiated by Jerry Lewis. I made a lot of pictures with Jerry—just bit parts—and if you salvaged all the film on the cutting-room floor you could make a full-length feature from my missing scenes. Anyway, that's how we got together.

One day Jerry calls me from his home. He's leaving for work and dropping off his young son, Gary, who is nine or ten.

"Whit, what's coming up on the air?" Jerry asks. "I'm taking Gary to school and I want him to think I'm magic."

"Well," I said, "there's two more records by the time you get into your car. Then I'll have two commercials and then a Como record."

"Great," he said, "now here's what I want you to do . . ."

Segue to Lewis's car tooling down Sunset Boulevard with son Gary beside him and both occupants listening to Old Loudmouth.

"Son, did you know that I'm *magic*?"

"Sure, Dad."

"Really. I'm magic."

"What do you mean?"

(The Como record is just ending.)

"See that radio, Gary?"

"Yeah."

"Watch!"

Jerry pointed at the car radio and yelled "Kaaa-ZAAM!"

And your Hollywood disc jockey came over the speaker with mysterious ghostly tones: "Garrrrry Lewwwwwwisss . . . You are on the way to schoolll . . . You had Post-Toasties for breakfast . . ."

Now the little fellow is looking around and smiling in wonderment.

"You are wearing a brown shirt and gray trousers . . ."

Later Gary's father called from the studio to say that Gary went out of his mind. Loved it. Made Jerry a big hero. Made a big fool out of Whittinghill.

We did it again later on, but this time I was the Tooth Fairy when Gary lost one of his teeth.

Just the other day I did Magic Mouth again and I hear it turned out better than I'd planned. The instigator was Cal Howard of Walt Disney Studios. Cal's a real funster and he actually looks like one of the cartoon characters. It's about 6:45 A.M. when Cal calls on my private line.

"My neighbor," he says, "is out in his garage and he's got you on real loud. And he's pounding nails into something. Damn fool is waking up the whole neighborhood. Take care of him, will you, Whit?"

"Leave it to me," I said.

Here's the tableau: Cal's neighbor, let's call him Fred Smith, is up on a little ladder pounding nails into the wall. I'm on his portable radio on the workbench. "Freeeeeeddddd Smmmmmmittthhhh . . . Fred Smmmittthhhh. Fred Smith! Stop pounding those nails and turn down your radio, you are driving everybody in the neighborhood nuts! This is the ghost of the hunter who shot Bambi! That is all . . ."

Cal later reported that Fred's hammer flew in the air and he stumbled off his ladder and ran around in circles for a few seconds. Then turned off his radio and ran in the house.

I really enjoy being a show business sophisticate.

30

Stems

WHILE I WAS GOING TO BOOK PARTIES and autograph sessions trying to hype (as they say in Hollywood) my first book, Alex Haley's *Roots* was going big. He was at the top of the best-seller list and I was No. 10 at the time on the Southern California hit parade.

After Tom Wayman had mentioned on his 7:30 P.M. newscast that Haley had drawn such big crowds at an autograph signing in Fox Hills, I came on with an off-the-cuff announcement that my second book, *Stems*, was coming out in the fall.

In *Stems*, I went on, I had researched my family through several generations and found out some very interesting things about my origins. The gag was terribly obvious, even for me.

I said that there were a few horse thieves in the family tree, and a town drunk and two village idiots. My grandmother, I said, was a mucker in the mines in Butte. She just stayed down in a copper mine and mucked all day. As far as I knew, in real life, Grandma had never been near Butte. But this was outrageous, as I said.

127

Great-grandmother, I reported, was captured by an Indian tribe in northern Montana and she was forced to travel with them. Her job was to sit outside the chief's wigwam and chew on his moccasins.

Each day, I gave more history of my origins, which would be forthcoming in *Stems*. (Great-grandma finally escaped and took up with a snake-oil salesman who ran a freak show on the side in Pocatello, Idaho.)

Unbelievably, a week hadn't gone by when I started receiving some *serious* mail about *Stems*.

One lady from Gardena wrote: "Ha, ha! You didn't write no such book. You are just stealing from Alex Haley. Who cares about your life? You stole the idea and it isn't going to sell."

I couldn't believe it. I thought my listeners were much more sophisticated than that!

But then comes a letter from a Ph.D. in Long Beach. A professor! And he says he agrees with the lady from Gardena, that I stole the idea from Alex Haley. He also says no one would care about a *disc jockey's* ancestors. But the bottom line was the stunner. This professor claims there's nothing in *Stems* but lies—get this, because he's *read* it!

But happily, just when I was ready to turn in my turntable, the *other side* started writing in. Thank the Lord for my regular listeners. Many of them began working on the movie rights and submitting their ideas for the cast. You know, Helen Twelvetrees and Conway Tearle. Or Zasu Pitts and Nels Asther. And someone suggested that the Ph.D. from Long Beach direct it since he was the only guy who's read it.

And the nicest thing that happened to *Stems* was a big silver plaque sent to me by the Trophy Room in Woodland Hills congratulating me for the third printing of *Stems*. My audience always comes to the rescue, bless them.

And if that lady from Gardena will come by KMPC, she can kiss my plaque.

31

Nat (King) Cole

NAT COLE was one of the truly great singers and one of the truly great gentlemen.

Shortly after I began my morning show on KMPC, Nat came out with a nice tune—part of an album, I believe—called "I'm Walkin' Out the Door." It seemed to be a perfect closing theme for me, and I've been using part of it at the end of my daily outrage for about 26 years.

My last line is always, "Thank you very much for listening, now if you'll excuse me . . ."

And Nat comes in with, "I'm walkin' out the door, with you on my mind . . ." (Fade under into newscast.)

I'd been using it for a few months when I ran into Nat at a cocktail party at Capitol Towers in Hollywood. It was the usual thing: agents, arrangers, musicians, singers, record-pluggers, etc. I was having a little sauce and I spot Nat over in a corner by himself. So I glide over and stick out my hand.

"Whataya say, Dick," Nat said, warmly (he talked as pretty as he sang).

"Doin' fine, Nat," I said. "Have you heard the show lately? I mean, have you heard the musical tag I'm using?"

"Yes, I have."

I was proud that Nat Cole listened to the show.

"One thing, Dick. I think it's great that you're using my tune. But how come you never play all of the record?"

He smiled broadly and I promised I would play it all.

And I have played it through a few times over the years.

I still play a lot of Nat Cole's music. Some of it sends chills up my spine.

How that man could sing a love song.

32

Happy Anniversary . . . (to Willy, Big Em, Big Red and Spooky Ol' Alice)

AFTER YOU'VE BEEN MARRIED as long as I have (41 years), it becomes more difficult each year to select the proper gift for the wife. I've been through the diamond, ruby, silver, paper, candlelight-and-wine, and moonlight-becomes-you bit. So when we got to our 40th, I began thinking about how I could really surprise my darlin', faithful, patient Willy.

I brought the question up at Lakeside. Where else?

We had adjourned to the dining room after a hard day on the golf course. At the round table were Jim Cross, the auto dealer; Jerry Priddy, former major league infielder; George Gobel, closet comedian, and Old Loudmouth.

I mentioned my upcoming wedding anniversary—the big four-zero—and my problem of selecting something different. Coincidentally, Jim, Jerry, and George all had wedding anniversaries coming up in close proximity. They all agreed it was time to come up with something besides a wristwatch or a set of china, or orchids and champagne.

"Every time I get Alice something," Gobel said, "she always returns it. So last year I gave her a quart of scotch. She didn't care for it, but I sure enjoyed it."

Somehow I got the brilliant notion, and everyone agreed—a billboard. A big sign saying happy anniversary to our wives! They'd get such a kick out of it.

I wasted no time getting on the phone to John Asher, KMPC's promotion man, who has one of the sharpest minds in the business.

Asher in turn phoned Foster and Kleiser, probably the largest billboard company in the country. And soon it was all arranged. We had our sign, and in a prime location on North Hollywood's fashionable Moorpark Street.

In about a week we were out inspecting it. We were so proud as we stood under it. It was spectacular, a huge thing:

FOUR GRATEFUL HUSBANDS WANT TO THANK WILLY, BIG EM, BIG RED, AND SPOOKY OL' ALICE FOR OVER 100 YEARS OF WEDDED BLISS.
DICK WHITTINGHILL, JIM CROSS, JERRY PRIDDY, GEORGE GOBEL—

"Even Alice ought to like this," George giggled.

"Big Em will die laughing," Cross said.

"This'll bust her up," Priddy chuckled.

"Willy will think I'm out of my mind," I said.

The next evening Willy is in the kitchen fixing dinner and I can't stand it any longer, even though our anniversary is several weeks away.

"Honey," I call, "get your coat on, we're going for a drive. I've got to show you something."

"I can't now, Whit, I'm busy."

"Honey, we have to go right now, it's a funny thing and you'll get a big laugh."

Well, I'm all smiles and can't wait for her reaction, because I know she's going to get a big giggle out of it. So we zoom up Riverside Drive and Willy is giving me this he's-getting-goofier-every-day look, and we get almost right under the sign and I stop.

"Why did you stop here?"

"Just look up there, Willy."

Slowly, she reads the sign, eyes widening.

I'm waiting for the laughter.

No laughter.

Tiny tears.

33

What if . . . ?

TRADE ITEM appearing in *Daily Variety* in the early fifties:

> Comedian Johnny Carson to New York to become host of
> the new teleseries, "Do You Trust Your Wife?" KMPC deejay
> Dick Whittinghill was offered the job but decided to remain on
> the West Coast.

What if . . . ?

.

34

Walkin' Out . . .

WE'RE COMING to the end again, and I feel a little like a person who is about to die and his whole life flashes before him. (And with my luck, someone else's life would flash before me.)

Well, a bunch of things are flashing through my mind now. Going far back, like writing *fuck* in the snow when I was in the second grade because one of my buddies told me to. I can still feel my teeth chattering as the female principal, a regular character out of Dickens, was shaking the life out of me. It wasn't until I was a freshman in high school that I found out what I'd written in the snow meant. . . .

And then the governor of Montana gave me a silver bugle for being the best Boy Scout bugler in the state; I was up on a stage, and my family was in the audience . . . And I remember saving coupons from selling the *Saturday Evening Post* to own a Scout uniform. Then it finally arrived and I put it on and walked proudly downtown in a pouring rain to show it off to my dad. Then, standing before him, almost crying, as the uniform—from the hat to the puttees—had shrunk at least three sizes . . .

I remember my first job: bugler and assistant cook at a Girl Scout camp! They wouldn't let me leave the kitchen area for two whole weeks because they thought I'd peek into the tents. And little did they know, I would have . . . I remember playing in the Helena High School State Championship Band; we won it three years in a row. And I recall the day I was to play in the contest for best trumpet player and watching the first contestant in front of me sucking on a lemon. You have no idea what that can do to a trumpet player . . .

Making the high school football team, only to break a leg in my senior year . . . Joining Sigma Chi at the University of Montana, and I'll never forget my initiation. Where some fraternities have one week as a *hell week*, we had to go for two —because one of the fellows told his girl friend about it . . .

And, of course, winning the university featherweight boxing championship and having to be pushed back into the ring for the extra round, which was required for the decision . . . Then I was quietly asked to leave the university because of a little prank. I drove a herd of cows down University Avenue up on the quad to graze while still wearing a tuxedo from the night before . . . Charging long-distance calls to my dad only to be told by the phone company manager I had to pay for them. Then getting a job in a hotel saloon playing trumpet to pay the phone bill . . .

Enrolling in dramatic school one block from what is now KMPC, and meeting another student, Gene Autry . . . Joining the Four Esquires and singing in amateur contests at local theaters . . . Working in my first movie, *Top of the Town*, for RKO . . . Then merging with the Rhythm Kings and Jo Stafford to form the Pied Pipers . . .

Then singing with the Pipers on the Alice Faye-Hal Kemp show for Chesterfield . . . then the Hollywood Hotel with Louella Parsons . . . then Jack Oakie's College of Musical

Knowledge with Stu Erwin . . . the Fred Allen Show . . . Bob Hope Show . . .

And the most important thing in my life, my marriage to my college sweetheart, Wilamet Matson. If I hadn't married her, I'd have been nothing but a bum . . . Then going all the way to New York for a one-night audition for Tommy Dorsey's program for Kool and Raleigh. The Pipers winning the audition but being laid off later when Dorsey temporarily disbanded his band . . . And looking for a job all over New York, and not finding one . . . Then returning to Helena, depressed and defeated, to take a job in the state auditor's office as assistant state fire marshal, of all things . . .

Forming my own 12-piece band to play at the Marlowe Theater in Helena and around town on weekends . . . Getting into radio at KPFA, Helena, for no salary. Working at the auditor's office during the day and then running down to the radio station to work from 6:00 P.M. to midnight . . . Landing an audition in Denver for KFEL, the Mutual Network station . . . Then getting fired after locking the owner in his office with a girl overnight . . .

Going into the Army under the Volunteer Officer's Corps . . . Then training black troops at Camp Phillips, Kansas. And it was off to New Guinea, where we built the greatest still this side of the Great Smokies . . .

After the war, it was back to California and a job on Glendale's KIEV. Getting fired at KIEV, and on to KGFJ. Leaving KGFJ and finally to KMPC, which was owned by an old dramatic school friend. It was a nice place and I stayed for 27 years . . .

During my years at KMPC, I've worked in more than 50 movies and TV series, worked at KTTV (Channel 11) and KNBC (Channel 4) doing afternoon movies and evening variety shows . . . Had parts in such shows as "Dragnet," "Bonanza," "Perry Mason," "Adam-12," "Ozzie & Harriet," "Emergency," "Switch," etc., etc.

After all the loudmouthing and silly stuff, the Kid from Montana was notified just recently that he has been chosen as one of 20 Significant Sigs from all over the United States to be honored for his contributions to whatever, I don't know. But I'm deeply touched and honored. Imagine, my own fraternity, Sigma Chi, honoring *me*! The list of Significant Sigs includes doctors, congressmen, former senators, presidents of universities, and corporate board chairmen . . . And at the bottom, listed alphabetically, is Dick Whittinghill, *disc jockey*.

I can't begin to tell you how much fun this has been. Imagine, not one but *two* books on *my* life. The Kid from Montana. Old Loudmouth. But, sadly, this is for sure. There won't be a third one. This is it. From now on, folks, it's Memory Lane and thanks for them. The record's over. I'm off the playlist. I'm tuning myself out.

OK, Nat, theme up and out:

"I'm walkin' out the door / With you on my mind . . ."

With you *always* on my mind.

Index